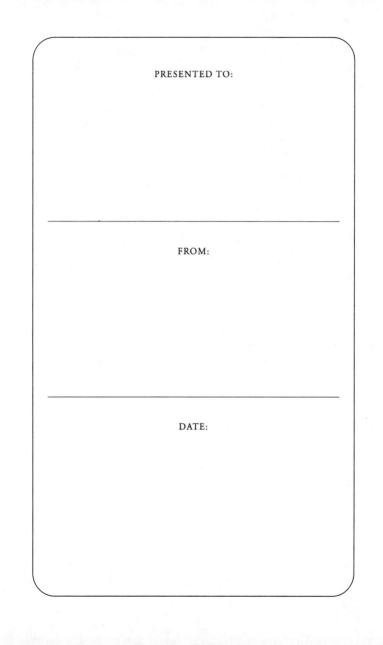

PRESENTED TO:

_____

FROM:

_____

DATE:

Other books by Michele Howe

Pilgrim Prayers for Single Moms
Going It Alone: Meeting the Challenges
  of Being a Single Mom

Forthcoming books by Michele Howe

Prayers for Homeschool Moms
Prayers of Comfort and Strength
Prayers for New and Expecting Moms

Prayers

to

Nourish a Woman's Heart

Prayers
to
Nourish a Woman's
Heart

Michele Howe

JOSSEY-BASS
A Wiley Imprint
www.josseybass.com

Jossey-Bass books and products are available through most bookstores. To contact Jossey-Bass directly call our Customer Care Department within the U.S. at 800-956-7739, outside the U.S. at 317-572-3986 or fax 317-572-4002.

Jossey-Bass also publishes its books in a variety of electronic formats. Some content that appears in print may not be available in electronic books.

Unless otherwise noted, the Scripture quotations contained herein are from the New American Standard Bible®, Copyright © 1960, 1962, 1963, 1968, 1971, 1973, 1975, 1977, 1995 by The Lockman Foundation. Used by permission. (www.Lockman.org)

Library of Congress Cataloging-in-Publication Data
Howe, Michele.
Prayers to nourish a woman's heart / Michele Howe.–1st ed.
p. cm.
Includes bibliographical references.
ISBN 0-7879-6581-2 (alk. paper)
1. Christian women–Prayer-books and devotions–English. I. Title.
BV4844.H68 2003
242'.843–dc21
2002155635

FIRST EDITION

HB Printing   10 9 8 7 6 5 4 3 2 1

Contents

Part Three: Overcoming Obstacles and Discouragement

Part Four: Facing Fears

Part Five: Discovering Joy and Satisfaction

To my grandmother, Rose Meyers, who loved me.

Acknowledgments

*T*hroughout my life, I have been immeasurably blessed with countless female friends, relatives, and work associates who never cease to add richness and value to my life. Truly, each of these precious ladies is a treasure of rare quality. It is their stories, as well as my own, that I am privileged to tell in this book of prayers for women. Over the years, I've been touched by these ladies' courage, reliance, and faith. I've watched in awe as each one has overcome tremendous personal pain and obstacles only to emerge more committed to investing themselves in the lives of others. Whether by choice or circumstance, these ladies have traveled difficult roads but all of life's brutalities have not overcome their inner character. Rather, all of them are more beautiful and polished because of the trials they've endured. To every one of these women, I offer my deepest gratitude. You are my heroes!

I would also like to express my gratitude to my editor at Jossey-Bass, Mark Kerr, another God-ordained instrument of blessing in my life. It is nigh on a miracle to me that I have been privileged to work with Mark and his team at Jossey-Bass. I am continually amazed at their expertise and wise counsel. Special thanks go to Andrea Flint, production editor; Sandy Siegle, marketing manager; and

Paula Goldstein, director, creative services. Working with such a gifted group of individuals has been an honor and a delight. Our mutual desire is that this selection of prayers will draw women from all walks of life closer to the One who alone can abundantly, beyond all hope and measure, meet every need and give a joy untouched by life's troubles and trials.

Prayers
to
Nourish a Woman's Heart

PART ONE

Limited Resources

Despite the best intentions, women who care about meeting the needs of others frequently find themselves struggling to keep pace with the demands made upon them. Any number of "shortages" can defuse even the most stalwart woman's determination to serve those she loves. Be it waning energy, financial issues, health concerns, or time crunches, every woman can discover hope amid even the most disheartening circumstances. As women take time to look upward, above, and beyond the trials, heavenly grace and strength will be both accessible and abundant.

Power Outage

ifty-three-year-old Catherine Wilson blew out her breath hard in an unconscious attempt to expel the worries of the day. As a secretary to the superintendent of the local public school system, Catherine came home daily one tired lady. It's not that she didn't enjoy her work. Catherine was a whiz when it came to organization, so this job was a Godsend. She was a natural with people too—which might be why so many of her elderly neighbors came knocking on Catherine's door whenever they had problems understanding a new prescription, Medicare information, or just simple banking account procedures.

After having been married for over twenty-seven years, Catherine just always assumed her husband would be around for the duration. She didn't count on an unexpected heart attack, which claimed his life and forever altered hers. But the unimaginable had happened and Catherine was left forging a new life for herself, by herself. The move into this new condominium complex for "older" adults was just the first in a series of life changes following her husband's death. Although Catherine didn't really qualify for senior status yet, she knew the time would arrive when she'd be grateful to have no more lawn care and home maintenance responsibilities. It was enough to keep up with her fast-paced position at school. Evenings were for taking care of chores, making dinner, exercising, and relaxing.

Lately though, in fact every night for the past week, Catherine's doorbell rang within the first hour she arrived home. How Catherine had earned the reputation of "mother superior" to all these truly elderly men and women who were her neighbors she couldn't fathom. It had started out with one innocent offer to act as go-between for the seventy-eight-year-old single lady with the beginnings of Parkinson's disease. All Catherine had done was to make a couple of telephone calls for her new friend. Then word spread that Catherine alone understood the ins and outs of getting real answers to difficult medical questions.

Sitting back in her comfy sofa, Catherine sighed again. *I wonder who'll be knocking on my door tonight? I'd like just one evening here alone,* Catherine thought wearily. *Still, these people have done something for me I never thought would happen again. I feel like I've got family, someone to come home to in the evenings. Maybe our friendships are somewhat lopsided, I do the advice giving and they do all the taking. But I'm also certain I fall far short of the gratefulness extended to me each and every time I make the effort to serve.*

"In everything I showed you that by working hard in this manner you must help the weak and remember the words of the Lord Jesus, that He Himself said, 'It is more blessed to give than to receive.'"
—ACTS 20:35

Dear Lord, today I learned something. I've been focusing on keeping so busy I won't notice how alone I feel and I've been wrong. No two ways about it. I can't run away from my hurt. I want to keep everyone at bay—push people away from me. Instead, I've been placed in a position where I don't have the choice to say no. Tired as I am, you're still forcing me to get out, move on, and heal inside. Should I be thanking you, Lord? I'm so emotionally worn out I don't want to get too close again. It just hurts too much. Then I look around and see the wrinkled brows, the stooped shoulders, and I realize I'm not the only one carrying a burden. Mine's just internal.

Lord, help me to give even when I don't have it within me to do so. Provide me with that greater measure of compassion I've been running from. I need your touch of grace and your ongoing strength to work through me. In the quietness of my heart, I hear you. Please help me do what is right. We all long for what you alone can offer. Let me be your conduit of tender love today. Amen.

Be as friendly to the janitor as you are to the chairman of the board.
—H. JACKSON BROWN JR. AND ROSEMARY C. BROWN IN *Life's Little Instructions from the Bible*

2

The Better Half

Jean, mother of three grown children, was hurrying to her sister Mary's home some forty miles south of her own town. Jean was once again rushing because Mary's doctor appointment was only one hour from now. Although the physician's office was close to Mary's house, Jean was seasoned with caring for her sister. She knew it often took fifteen to twenty minutes just to get Mary ready to leave and out the door to the car. *If only I hadn't taken that phone call,* Jean fretted. *I know how much Mary hates to be late to these appointments—anywhere for that matter. Lord, how you took two people so opposite and stuck them in one family, I'll never understand. And us being twins to boot!*

Driving along the highway, Jean tried to calm herself but with Mary's check-up this morning and a full afternoon of errands to run for her sister after lunch, Jean felt exhausted. "I'm spent, worn out, no more energy," Jean said aloud to no one present. "God, help me. Mary's the one who been through the wringer. Cancer six years ago, then a recurrence last fall. She's just recovering now and her strength certainly isn't coming back like we'd hoped. I wonder if she'll ever be the same vivacious Mary we all knew?" Jean felt the burning behind her eyes. *I will not shed a single tear* today. That's all Mary needs is to see my emotional side kick into gear right before we head out. Oh, God, I don't know what it is that I'm lacking, but I definitely am in need. I'm so frazzled with everything that's happening. Nothing I've planned has worked out. This whole year has been full of unwanted news and bad surprises. Help me carry on through these next stressful months. I want to be there for Mary. Sometimes I just don't know how I'll manage it all.

Rejoicing in hope, persevering in tribulation, devoted to prayer.
—ROMANS 12:12

Dear Lord, there is a part of me too tired, too discouraged to pray. I don't want to spend my quiet moments with you whining, complaining, or worrying. I want to enter your presence full of thankfulness and so very aware of the many blessings you've bestowed on my life. Yet my heart is so heavy. I am burdened within and without. Life just seems too difficult for me now. I am hurting more deeply than I ever recall. The irony is that it's not me who's suffering. It's someone I love more than life. And there's nothing I can do to ease her pain. I can hold her hand, listen to her speak, and cry with her. But I feel so out of control. Nothing prepares me for the bad reports the doctor doles out with such regularity. If anything, I'm the one who's being ministered to. Something is askew here. I want to be the strong one. I have to be there for my loved one. Lord, why did you form me so weak? Why am

I so fragile? They're counting on me to be strong and steadfast. Lord, I'm not able to carry this burden. Will you? Show me how to hand over the hardships I'm struggling with to you. In my heart, I realize this is something I should have done long ago. But, no. I tried to be the mighty one, the pillar of strength. And how long did that last Lord? A few months maybe? I beg you to take away my fears, my distress, and my worrisome heart. Remake me. Give me your peace and the reassurance I long for. I understand that I will not be privy to the future and that is a blessing in itself. Still, I must know that you are caring for those I love. I have to have confidence that everything you do—you do well. Hold me close today, Lord. Minister to me in my frailty and lift me up. Amen.

> *God always seems bigger to those who need him most. And suffering is the tool he uses to help us need him more.*
> —JONI EARECKSON TADA WITH STEVEN ESTES IN *Christianity: A Follower's Guide*

The Jitters

*C*aught between taking care of her three children and her parents' needs, Terry, a forty-four-year-old single mom of two sons and a daughter, gripped the steering wheel with a vengeance. En route to the fifth grocery store of the morning, and for a box of Jell-O no less, Terry felt about ready to explode. Be reasonable, calm down, demonstrate patience, Terry repeated over and over. This is the last stop, I can do this. I can make it through the next few hours without losing self-control. Attempting to still the uproar in her emotions, Terry prayed for God to give her the kind words and gentle attitude she knew her mom needed right now. But it wasn't easy.

The last three years had revealed just how frail and needy Terry's father had become. At last, after frequent family discussions, Terry's parents agreed that the current living arrangement wasn't working. Terry was running herself ragged trying to maintain her own home and take care of her parents' yard and house as well. Even with three teens to assist her, Terry's resources were running dangerously low. Finally, a decision had been agreed upon. Terry would move in with her parents. Their sprawling house and acres of farm land would be perfect for her kids' last years at home. Terry looked forward to selling her smaller home and investing the revenue from the sale. Each day, Terry found new positives about moving in with her folks, where caregiving wouldn't require long distance phone conversations or forty-five minute travel time. Still, after patiently playing chauffeur to her mother all morning, Terry was having second thoughts. What ifs loomed large. *If today is a sample of how I'll react to my mom's requests, can I handle living with both Mom and Dad around the clock?* Terry then experienced a squirm in her stomach that cautioned her to take a deep breath and say another prayer.

For He Himself is our peace.
—EPHESIANS 2:14A

Dear Lord, thank you for your abundant care for my family and me. Over the years, I've come to recognize your tender touch more readily. You've helped me listen with ears that truly hear your voice. I am so grateful for your guiding hand, your rod of protection. Lord, I praise you. In the innermost depths of my soul, I bow to your holiness. It is a good thing to give praise to you, my God. In every circumstance, you have shown yourself faithful to meet my every need. And now, I come again, asking for your wisdom, your perspective. I am wrestling with an issue that is unclear to me. While I am certain of the right step to take, I am concerned that I don't have what it takes to fulfill my responsibilities. Today, when confronted with demands I felt were unreasonable, I did not handle it well. Instead of communicating with honesty, I held back and allowed bitterness and anger to well up inside me. It was not a pretty picture. Even now as I recall the episode, I bristle. Lord, will you give me a heart of service? Demonstrate to me how important it is to lay down my life in countless small ways every day. I am in sore need of your touch of grace. I feel ashamed that I still tend to react with selfish intent. Please extend to me your good word of encouragement. I do ask your forgiveness for resisting the grace you offered me earlier. Grace to do good without grumbling. In the future, teach me to handle difficult situations, difficult people, with honesty and forthrightness. Be my guide as I make more feeble attempts at serving others with the same bountiful spirit of abandonment that Christ demonstrated with those he served. I commit my life, my hands, and my feet to your service. In these coming days, let your goodness and grace be the watchword of my life. Amen.

In His [Jesus'] last message before His death, He wanted you and me to comprehend with our whole being that He has left us on this planet for one compelling reason—and it has everything to do with fruit.
—Bruce Wilkinson in *Secrets of the Vine*

4
The Sweetest Song

Perched atop her hospital bed overlooking the now-neglected garden, Lauren continued to rue the day she entered her friend's beauty salon. All for the sake of vanity, she mumbled disgustedly. Though the sun was shining and the birds were chirping merrily as they built their spring homes, nothing lifted Lauren's sour mood. I am trying to maintain a positive attitude, I really am, Lauren's eyebrows lifting as if to persuade herself. This is just too much for any sane person to take. First I fall over a roller, break my foot and end up in a cast for six weeks. Now, I find out my foot hasn't knit itself back together and the doctor is suggesting surgery. No way. I'll just sit it out for another two weeks and we'll see. Even if I had the surgery done tomorrow, I wouldn't be any help to Lindsay when she moves upstate. I want to be there right along with everyone else, helping my only daughter move into her first home. I know it's nothing earth-shattering, but Lord, I do want to be a part of this new juncture for Lindsay. I need to be there, to see that she gets settled properly. And I believe she wants me there too. But no, I'm lying here, being a good patient . . . in body at least, trying to mend myself, but I feel so frustrated. I want to get up, I have a thousand little errands to run, and all the extra surprises I had planned to make Lindsay's last weeks at home are pointless now. Lord, help me here. I'm running myself ragged without moving a muscle. Everywhere I look, I see another task that needs tending to and still here I sit. Alone. Everyone else is out doing something productive, except me. If I can't "do" anything, what else is there?

A sudden wash of shame swept over Lauren. Forgive me, Lord, you really do know how to shake a girl up. Prayer—the sweetest song, the most important task of all, and I'd forgotten.

Therefore, confess your sins to one another, and pray for one another, so that you may be healed. The effective prayer of a righteous man can accomplish much.
—JAMES 5:16

Dear Lord, how shall I begin? You are already so very aware of my internal conflicts. You see my struggles and hear my pleas. Still, amazingly, you love me. You beckon me to come close and love you as well. Lord, I ask your forgiveness for my attitude of ungratefulness. I am so grieved that I continue to run circles around myself in my feeble attempts to feel better about my circumstances. I want to know that everything will be as I planned. Yet life is too untamable! Nothing is ever guaranteed. I realize that even though my calculated plans may not come to pass in the way I imagined them, I can still offer my service in a far more valuable way. I can pray. While I long to be in the midst of the "action," I understand that your promises tell us that as we pray much can be accomplished. Lord, let it be so. Accomplish much through my prayers. Teach me how to pray according to your will and let the power be released from the heavens to bring honor and glory to you. Thank you for the lessons you are teaching me even now. I am learning, though slowly I admit, to sit quietly at your feet. To rest in the knowledge that you are present with me, with those I love, every minute. This comforts me greatly. Though I am unable to carry on with my own work, I willingly choose to labor in prayer for your people. Guide my thoughts, my words. I ask that you do your work and give me the privilege to be a part of this grand story called life. One day, I believe each of us will truly understand just how significant our tiny portions were. Thank you again for loving me back to the truth, for giving me another chance to draw near to you. I praise you, Lord, you are wonderful. You are my God and the reason for my song. Amen.

Although power can force obedience, only love can summon a response of love, which is the one thing God wants from us and the reason he created us.
—PHILIP YANCEY IN *The Jesus I Never Knew*

5

Pipe Dreams

hirty-three-year-old Becky was a single mom to ten-year-old Travis, whom she adored with every ounce of her being. Trucking through their rented house, Travis frequently stopped midstride and would backtrack over to where Becky was working around the home to stop and give her a giant-sized hug. "I love you, Mom," were words Becky heard frequently. Today, Saturday, was catch-up on the chores day around their house, so Becky was flitting from one task to the next in the hopes she'd be done before her parents arrived to take them out for pizza that afternoon. And a movie besides! Becky was elated. It had been quite some time since she'd had the extra pocket money to treat Travis to a dinner out and a movie as well. Becky was grateful her folks often came through in such fun ways, knowing that Becky didn't have the cash for many extras.

Working around diligently, Becky started sorting through Travis's clothes for school. So many looked ragged now that December had arrived. Even his shoes were scuffed up and showing wear. Well, maybe this year clothes will be the Christmas gift, Becky mused. Carrying the load of clothes she'd just finished drying into her kitchen, Becky began sorting and folding, her mind continually drawn back to Travis and his clothes. Why do I feel so bad getting my son necessities for his Christmas present? I'd love to get him new computer games, maybe some roller blades . . . but I can't. I can't afford it. Seems like I say, "We can't," more and more all the time. I know I should be thankful we have a home, a car, enough to eat, but there's this niggling dissatisfaction in the back of my mind. I do want to give my son more—of everything. Lord, help me overcome the American "gimme" syndrome. We have so much, please remind me how very blessed I am despite a pocketbook that's fraying around the edges.

<hr/>

But godliness actually is a means of great gain, when accompanied by contentment.
—1 TIMOTHY 6:6

Dear Lord, I need an accelerated lesson in contentment. Not just for today, but for every day. Not simply for my family's needs, but for every aspect of my life. Too often, I confess, I'm walking around contemplating how I might squeeze more from my paycheck. I look for ways to put "more stuff" into our lives. Lord, I am not a content woman. I cannot recall a time when I was completely overwhelmed with your love alone. And yet that is where I long to be! I hunger to be at rest deep within my heart where outside matters won't pull me away from you. More than any "thing," I desire to be at peace within my soul and to graciously accept the life you've given me. Whether or not I ever have the resources I desire to give to my loved ones is beside the point. This lesson of contentment is one my family would do well to learn, too. It is freeing to live life not wanting more, to be grateful for what good things you have already given, not expecting blessings around every corner. I mistakenly believe that if I have more to give that our lives will be better. Yet I know that money and the power it exudes can tear families apart. I've seen this happen. Protect us from this danger, Lord. Keep us well within the bounds of your protection.

Lord, the only blessing we can rightfully ask of you is the blessing of your presence, your power in our lives. Draw near to me today and bless me! I want to sense your nearness to me every hour, and I delight in being your child. You are the one who created, nurtured, and protected me. You continue to see to my every need. Thank you. Open my eyes and teach me how to walk in the light of your love. Let my life be an example for my child. Lord, let me see the true riches, the treasure of your love. Amen.

Money separates people more often than it joins them.
—Liz Curtis Higgs in *Bad Girls of the Bible*

6

Incomplete

$\mathcal{S}$itting in the ICU waiting area, Melissa tried in vain to concentrate on the packet of information given her by the attending physician. She knew this day was fast approaching, but knowing it was barreling toward her didn't make accepting it any easier. Melissa's husband of twenty-nine years was going through the most challenging chapter of his life thus far. Diabetes had reared its ugly head some fifteen years previous. Jon had thought he only had a bad case of a flu virus. When they'd taken him to the doctor's office, further tests revealed diabetes. At first, it didn't appear that Jon's lifestyle would be much affected. He did change his eating habits some, exercised more, and checked his blood sugar levels several times a day. All in all, Melissa thought Jon would handle this disease and overcome it. He was that kind of guy. But now, Melissa could see how ill-informed she had been, how naive. People didn't just "get over" something as serious as diabetes. Sure, they could lower their risk, pay careful attention to make certain they were doing all they could to prevent any further complications, but unless a cure arose, or God healed, diabetes would be their lifelong companion.

So as the months and years passed, Jon found it more and more difficult to get his sugar levels in the range his doctor wanted. Then other health issues started to rise. After several weeks of fighting a hangnail turned rogue, Jon's foot was infected. Antibiotics helped, but then Jon's foot became more painful. The infection had reached deep within the muscle tissue and into his bone. After more weeks of unsuccessfully fighting this terror, the doctors told Jon his foot would have to come off. Melissa was trying hard to accept this latest blow, trying to be brave for Jon's sake. But inside she felt like a part of her was dying. How would she rise to the challenge of caring for Jon as an amputee? Of course, this didn't change how she felt about Jon. No, Melissa was just plain scared. Nothing seemed certain, let alone manageable any longer.

Whoever speaks, let him speak, as it were, the utterances of God; whoever serves, let him do so as by the strength which God supplies; so that in all things God may be glorified through Jesus Christ, to whom belongs the glory and dominion forever and ever.
—I PETER 4:11

Dear Lord, this is beyond my ability to cope. I beg you to come close beside me and hold me up—hold us up. To lose one's health is so very painful. Then to lose a part of one's body is devastating. I do not blame you Lord for not healing. I know that ours is a fallen, broken world where pain, illness, and suffering are close companions to us all. I only ask that you come along with us now. Give us your strength to live today. For right at this moment, even making it through the next hour is too difficult. Give me the right words to say to bring encouragement and assurance to this one I love. Help him see that this change in him won't affect how I care for him. Give him the grace to face the healing and the pain involved in this slow process. I pray you infuse him with a daily determination to stay at the task at hand. Let him not become discouraged at any setbacks that may arise. Lord, help him see that I stand with him through this nightmare. Give us a boost when we need it—a way to laugh, some outlet of joy to release all our pent-up emotions. As we face this newest challenge, teach us how to live in complete trust in you. Allow us to see your plan for our lives and continue to make us sensitive to the leading of your spirit. As we sit and wait upon you, I pray you refresh our downtrodden hearts. Make all things new again. Begin with our feeble faith and strengthen us even now. Amen.

> *Fear is a strange wind. It is not a wind that propels us forward, but a wild paralyzing one that puts us in a holding pattern.*
> —SHEILA WALSH IN *Living Fearlessly*

7

Shutting Down

*T*rue to form, the minute Sue Ann answered the telephone her three kids came clamoring for attention, advice, and to argue. It had been understandable when Sue Ann's children were toddlers and preschoolers—but now, at junior high and even high school age? Why, Sue Ann despaired, can't I have a moment alone? It seems the second I begin a task, sit down to concentrate on something, or am on the telephone these kids become my second skin.

Sue Ann, once endearingly nicknamed Sulky Sue, found it difficult to maintain a patient, calm demeanor these days. Though she dearly loved her children, Sue Ann herself noticed she was lapsing into her Sulky Sue mode more and more frequently. It didn't help that her kids needed her to drive them places at all hours. Even though Sue Ann wasn't changing diapers, nursing minor injuries, or brushing three sets of teeth twice daily, she still felt spent. Instead of the former physical exhaustion Sue Ann had experienced during the early mothering years, she now understood what emotional exhaustion meant. Sue Ann was depleted in every conceivable way. What made Sue Ann particularly vulnerable to the ups and downs so common to parenting preteens and teens was that her husband's promotion now meant he was traveling two days a week.

Suddenly Sue Ann felt as though life and its multitude of pressures was simply too much for her. She wanted to check out. Instead, Sue Ann did what all women should do when they feel as though they're drowning under a sea of other people's wants and needs; she called a friend and cried, "Help!" Thankfully for Sue Ann, her friend was home and responded to her frantic pleas.

He restores my soul.
—PSALM 23:3A

Dear Lord, I need a reprieve from life. I admit, this sounds selfish, maybe even a bit silly. But I'm drowning under this load of responsibilities. My loved ones need my advice, my input, and me every day—seemingly every hour. I'm just so worn out. I used to daydream about the time when diapers, dishes, and runny noses would no longer be the culmination of my day. Now, looking back, I see that perhaps serving in those ways was probably much simpler. I have tried to keep our family on a balanced course, not too fast, not too crazy. Yet life is crowding out my good intentions. Our family is veering into an out-of-control pace that dizzies me. Lord, help us, me in particular, to regroup and revisit each area of our lives. We need to set guidelines for our family in light of our long-term goals. The way we're headed now, I'm afraid we'll lose that which we hold most precious—our love for you. Please bring together all the loose ends that fill my thoughts, help me work through the difficulties and discard anything that stands in the way of living for you. You, Lord, have entrusted these wonderful children to me. Yet I'm seeing them more as a burden than a blessing. Forgive me. Remake my heart and refresh my soul so that I might give to my family from a heart that is full to overflowing. Open my eyes and give me a refined and purified love for them all. Show me how to be the mother I must be for them. I am your child, still on the learning curve myself. Continue to support me and give me your rest. I am so in need of a touch from you, Lord. This job is far too imposing for me. I must have you with me today and every day. For the sake of your good name and to bring honor to you, I ask that you continue to enable me to "put on" good works, positive attitudes, and a pleasant demeanor. Amen.

Your presence, your support, and your input may not be openly encouraged and will likely be resisted. But your involvement is an essential part of your early teen's social and spiritual development.
—CARLA BARNHILL IN *How to Parent Your Teen Without Losing Your Mind*

8

The Song That Never Ends

She's almost asleep, Joy whispered as she stroked her granddaughter's head contentedly. Rocking her for a few more minutes, Joy relished these tender, quiet moments with her only granddaughter. What a precious gift she was to Joy. Slowly, Joy gathered her ten-month-old granddaughter and gently placed her in the crib. Covering her with a light blanket, Joy flipped the baby monitor on high and eased the bedroom door shut. Joy took advantage of naptime to get a head start on her garden. She turned on the companion monitor and cinched it to her belt, grabbed her gardening gloves, and went to work. As Joy bent over her rose bed, she alternately weeded and pruned. Her sixty-some-year-old body wasn't up to constant bending anymore. But Joy was determined to continue her favorite hobby just as long as she was able. She knew she'd just have to learn to pace herself now that arthritis and tired bones were creeping in.

It was one of Joy's strongest assets, her persistence to make things happen. And thankfully, this character trait didn't apply only to work. If Joy hadn't been diligent in her pursuit of gaining temporary custody of her granddaughter, a foster home would have taken her. Joy was resolved to gain permanent custody of little Autumn if need be. Joy had shed many grievous tears over her son's lack of responsibility. It shouldn't have surprised her that he had impregnated a woman almost half his age who had absolutely no intention of being a mother to any man's child. Joy thought it miraculous that the girl carried Autumn to term and didn't abort her. In Joy's standard style, she was continuing to rely on God's provision to meet any needs that might arise for either her or Autumn. Joy knew of God's faithfulness and she counted on it every hour.

Not lagging behind in diligence, fervent in spirit, serving the Lord.
—ROMANS 12:11

Dear Lord, this is the hour which I long for each and every day. The time when you and I are alone and can converse together. I cannot conceive of a time more dear to me than these still and tranquil moments we share together. I thank you now that you allow your children access to the throne of grace. You hear my prayers and are close to my heart. Lord, today I am so very grateful for new life and the lives of my beloved family. I see new beginnings. Fresh opportunities to start over. I admit that I made many mistakes in my life. I do regret the lack of time I spent with family. I was too busy meeting the needs of other families and neglected my own.

No wonder that my loved ones are still in search of something stable to grasp hold of. I ask that you have mercy upon my family and me and draw them to you. I also pray that you will turn their hearts toward you. My spirit tells me to bask in your promises to supply my every need. My soul reminds me that you have never let me down. I must continue to feed my mind with the truth found in your words. Lord, I am honored to nurture those in my care and I ask that you bless their lives mightily. Surround them with your protective presence and keep all manner of evil far from them. I commit them to you today. Be with us, help us as we continue our journey toward heaven. Let our lives shine for you. Amen.

He [Jesus] forgives and He forgets. He creates and He cleanses. He restores and He rebuilds. He heals and He helps. He reconciles and He redeems. He comforts and He carries. He lifts and He loves.
—ANNE GRAHAM LOTZ IN *Just Give Me Jesus*

9

Hot Spots

*C*arefully calculating the amount of ingredients needed for each recipe was taking Vanessa much longer than she had anticipated. It was normally a fifteen- to twenty-minute job. Today already an hour had passed and Vanessa still wasn't done. As the town's only vocational school's head chef, Vanessa was in charge of implementing and managing the school's culinary arts program. Vanessa had at one time managed her own restaurant and loved every minute of it. But when the economy had taken a downturn her restaurant couldn't survive the competition from the larger chains of eateries popping up all over her small community. It was then that Vanessa decided to turn her talents to teaching. As a single woman without any children of her own, Vanessa had energy to spare. At this time, her life and her time were her own—which is why she accepted the position as the supervisor-manager-teacher for the entire culinary school within the technical college. Her students included both high school kids on a work-and-learn program and college-aged enrollees.

Vanessa's biggest challenge to date was incorporating both types of students into a single, streamlined program. She noted that the older participants were ready learners and more serious about developing skills to aid them in their careers. A handful of the high school students were a different story. Thinking that "cooking classes meant an easy ride, some enrolled only to discover how much diligence and skill it took to become a chef. Vanessa brainstormed ways to get these potentially "troubled" kids involved in her program. She designed a special incentive program to help. One Saturday a month, any student who signed up to help her plan, prepare, and serve a meal at the homeless shelter would receive extra points toward their grade. So far, Vanessa's plan was working. She noted a side benefit too; previously disinterested students were viewing life from a completely different angle and now were putting more effort into making something of themselves.

For Thou dost recompense a man according to his work.
—PSALM 62:12

Dear Lord, how can I best have an impact on these young lives to do their best? I want them to see the connection between giving a good day's work and finding satisfaction in accomplishing that alone. I'm afraid that some of them won't be successful. They are not lazy, but they lack the motivation to try. Somehow they've gotten the message that the world owes them and will take care of them. This is a scary scenario. As an adult, I understand that each person must work and work hard to earn his way. Yet how does this knowledge transfer to teens who live only for the moment? Lord, you are the master instructor. Help me find a method that bridges the gap between my generation and this one. Show me how to teach in a manner that will bring understanding. I want only the best for each of these youngsters. Be there for me as I attempt to break through this barrier that has been erected. I care deeply for every person who walks into my life. Give me the tools I need to engage their minds and to incite a passion for learning. Be my guide as I give to each person as his or her need requires. Help me see each one as an individual and treat each accordingly. As I continue to guide, provide me with the strength to keep plugging away in spite of any setbacks. Be here in our midst as we journey through this year. As I go to you daily for your wisdom and insight, remake me into a woman who brings honor to your name. My entreaty is that every person will walk away having learned about the realities of life and the blessing that hard work brings. Amen.

If our name rings up wonderful memories, positive thoughts, or remembrances of promises fulfilled, our character may be counted as priceless. If, on the other hand, our everyday essence reeks of selfishness or inconsistency or dishonesty, our name isn't worth a deflated dime.

—JOHN TRENT IN *Be There!*

PART TWO

Multitasking

*A*t home or at work, with family or friends, when healthy or ill, during good times and bad, women are called upon to perform a multitude of tasks and do them well. Women consistently summon up the finest of their gifts, talents, and resources to make others feel more cared for, comfortable, and content. Yet there are stretches of time when these women themselves require a good word, a helping hand, and a generous hug. May it be that all women exercise such goodwill toward one another in greater measure and in greater frequency to lessen each other's burden of care.

10

No One's Home

At 4:45 P.M., twenty-three-year-old Beth was reaching her peak stress management skills. Dinner was coming together, nicely for a change. The baby was howling for attention, no surprise there. And the telephone was ringing . . . again. Giving the chili one last stir and turning the burner down a bit lower, Beth grabbed the baby from his crib and dashed for the telephone. By the time she picked up the receiver, the line was dead. "Ugh," Beth mumbled. "Not again, Lord, please I don't think I'm up to playing the servant girl role today. Help me keep the next ten minutes in perspective, Lord, please."

Anticipating what was about to occur, Beth straightened her hair and kept watch from her kitchen window. Minutes later, Beth spied her elderly neighbor making his way to her back door. "Patience, Beth, patience," she said quietly. Steeling herself for another abrupt demand on her already busy schedule, Beth opened the door and invited her neighbor inside.

Ten minutes later, Beth had been handed a "to-do" list in short order. Looking over the crabby handwriting, Beth mentally checked off what she'd be doing the following morning after breakfast. There would be three doctor's appointments to be made, one call to the pharmacist, and another phone call to the senior center's home health care specialist. "That and groceries too," Beth complained.

I don't mind helping out, Beth thought silently. But a thank you once in a while might be nice. A simple request instead of a demand would be refreshing too. Don't expect the impossible, Beth told herself. Just try to remember how kind and courteous Old Joe was before he got cancer last year. That and three operations later, Beth sympathized. No wonder he's cranky, he's had three of his organs either removed or cut into in just over a year. He's afraid, Beth conceded. And I'm worn out. Still, a little in the way of gratefulness would sure be nice. And what about my life, Lord?

Owe nothing to anyone except to love one another; for he who loves his neighbor has fulfilled the law.
—ROMANS 13:8

Dear Lord, I make a claim I cannot back up. I say that I am your child. But when it comes down to living as Christ did, with all the service and the sacrifice, I am a sham. I complain to high heaven about how busy I already am. And still, I must be prepared to help my neighbor, my friend. Why is this so difficult for me? I am already feeling the pressure of maintaining my home and raising my family. It seems unreasonable that I am forced into a situation where I have to care for others at the same time. Isn't that supposed to come later in life? And with my own family? My own mom, dad, and grandparents? Please, Father, show me how to put aside these frustrations. I want time to myself. I want quietness and peace. I want . . .

There is the rub. I am in a constant state of "want." Lord, fill my heart, my mind, and my soul with your goodness. Take away my wants and replace them with your presence. I need to know you better. In my heart of hearts, I do desire to be the servant you require me to be. And to do this work with a humble heart, a grateful spirit even; one that recognizes it is a gift to be strong enough to serve. Change my outlook, Lord. Please renew a right spirit within me. Give me that zealous passion to seek out and gladly meet others' needs when you bring them to my door. Enlarge my smallish heart and open my eyes to the gift that youth epitomizes. Help me lavish love on those who are hurting and truly learn to do unto others as you would have me. Let me be your servant today and strengthen my resolve to love others with the same zeal Christ has revealed to us. Amen.

Cracked but laughing. Imperfect but hopeful. Flawed but happy. Broken but optimistic. Wounded but healing. Scarred but still capable of embracing joy.
—KAREN SCALF LINAMEN IN *Sometimes I Wake Up Grumpy . . . and Sometimes I Let Him Sleep*

II

On Call

$\mathcal{K}$elly, a mother of four, dialed the pediatrician's office for at least the sixth time. She inwardly winced as she pressed the redial button on her phone when the line signaled busy. Sitting cross-legged on the floor of her bedroom, speaking quietly, Kelly once again asked for the nurse on duty. After waiting another twelve minutes, the cheerful voice on the other end told Kelly she was indeed speaking to her favorite nurse in the large and ever burgeoning pediatric practice. *It's Kim, thank you, Lord,* Kelly said inwardly.

After explaining yet another time that her son, Jeremy, was still coughing up the yellow mucus, still fighting a drippy nose and frequent sinus pain, still coughing in general, Kelly felt tempted to demand another appointment. Instead, even her favorite, knowledgeable nurse told Kelly to be patient. "It's just a viral infection, no antibiotics are going to help Jeremy." Kelly was reminded how even the week previous, the x-ray showed that Jeremy's sinuses were totally clear. Hanging up the telephone, Kelly should have been relieved. A part of her did feel that way. Still, Kelly continued to knead her temples in exhaustion. *It's a fine thing for others to say, "Be patient," but poor Jeremy's about had it with being sick this long. Me too. I can't put* my finger on why I feel so down about this particular illness—maybe because it's lingered so long only to come back with a vengeance. Yet my son's not in the hospital, he's not terminally ill. He's just a sick kid. I have to remind myself of that. No, it's not fun being sick or the one who's playing nurse on call twenty-four hours a day. But that's my job as mom and by golly, we'll beat this thing yet.

Faithful is He who calls you, and He also will bring it to pass.
—1 THESSALONIANS 5:24

Dear Lord, you are a wonder to me. How you take two humans and create a new life and these two adults learn to give themselves to their offspring amazes me. It is a miracle that as selfish as I am, you continue to work in me to bring good to others in my care. Left to my own instincts, I would turn from this awesome responsibility, not because of the hardship, but because of the pain. It hurts me into the depth of my heart when my children suffer. I cannot fathom a pain that cuts deeper. Yet somehow you have worked your wonder of love within our hearts as mothers. We continue loving those around us despite the inner anguish we feel. Enduring our own pain is one thing, but being called on to shore up our kids when they're experiencing doubt and suffering is another task completely. Unless you, merciful God, bestow upon us your grace, which indeed supplies our every need, I am not able to press ahead. Even today, I became so bogged down by the complaints of my child. I understand how he feels, for I am experiencing the same emotions. But Lord, help me point his smallish mind to you. Show me how to direct my child's worries to your care.

I admit this small setback has me stymied. I sit and fret, frustrated that I am unable to remove even so small a sickness from my child. I don't want to see my loved one suffer any longer. Weariness tugs at my heart all throughout the day. Nights bring no relief. I am constantly reminded how transient this life is. There are no quick fixes, no guarantees of a healthy pain-free existence. Yet I long for the day when the world as we know it will be free from pain, from tears, from suffering. I ask you, Lord, to not delay. Come to my help, my aid. Give me what I require today to love without restraint. Make me your hands, your feet today. Embrace my hurting heart and replenish my desperate soul with your matchless grace. Amen.

All our emotional and spiritual resources are gone. And yet, somehow, we go on. It must be God, giving us his strength. This is the only explanation that makes sense.
—BRIAN SCHRAUGER IN *Walking Taylor Home*

12
No-Sleep Zone

Forty-six-year-old Dawn Wells didn't scream when her ten-year-old son gently tapped her on the shoulder at 2:00 A.M. wanting a dose of cough medicine. Dawn knew the routine all too well to be startled anymore. Rarely did she get a full night's sleep these days. With her son Matt waking her up at night for more medicine to help conquer his lingering cough aggravated by severe allergies, and the telephone calls from her parents needing immediate assistance, Dawn was spent. Too tired to say a word, she quietly made her way into the kitchen, took out the measuring spoon, and doled the cough syrup into her son's mouth. I've got to get some sleep, Dawn thought through bleary eyes and a foggy brain.

No sooner had Dawn placed her head back on her pillow when racing thoughts of her parents' needs started to well up in her mind. Dawn was facing a momentous decision about her parents' care alone. Her mom and dad finally accepted that they couldn't live alone any longer, but what was plan B? Either Dawn would invite them to move into her home with her family or they would rent an adult assisted living apartment way across town. Both ideas had their pros and cons. On the one hand, Dawn dreaded the thought of having to make a forty-five minute drive

several times a week to take her parents to their appointments, shop for groceries, or even simply run errands. On
the other hand, Dawn wasn't sure her husband and kids
were ready for Grandma and Grandpa to live with them
full time and vice versa. No doubt, there's going to be
adjustments for all of us whatever happens. Dawn tried to
come to a decision. Now fully awake, she was more than a
little anxious. This is crazy, she thought, and Dawn rolled
over and pounded her pillow into a comfortable ball. God,
what is the right answer? Not surprisingly, no bolt of light-
ening came, so Dawn prayed again. Lord, just give me the
peace I need to get some rest. Tomorrow will come soon
enough and then I'll trust you to help me make the best
choice for everyone involved.

Anxiety in the heart of a man weighs it down,
But a good word makes it glad.
—PROVERBS 12:25

Dear Lord, slow learner that I am, I look everywhere but to
you for what I need most—peace. I cannot live long in this
world without the good word from you that speaks peace to
my heart and soul. I admit to feeling troubled and concerned
about this decision I am facing. I try to gather all the facts,
take into consideration everyone's feelings, and yet I still am
unable to make a definitive choice. What is the matter with
me? Throughout the day, I am haunted by the gravity of this
whole situation. I am dealing with the lives of others and
they've placed the choice in my hands. Lord, somehow will

you instruct my mind? I require so much of your wisdom at this time. Without your guidance and support, I feel as though I'll just slip through the cracks. Nothing comes easily it seems, not even sleep. I am tossing and turning throughout the night. I wake up exhausted and even more compromised to handle the responsibilities of the day. Lord, turn my eyes again toward you. Remind me, gently please, how you care for my every need. Touch my soul with your goodness and your grace. Lift my burdens from me. I am not able to shoulder this weight any longer. I admit how very weak I am. Yet you are my provider. Your word feeds my soul with truth. Continue to prompt me to look to your precious promises every day and every night. Set the seal of your truth upon my heart. Lord, you do all things well. I do trust that with your hand guiding mine, we'll see this through to its completion. Amen.

The dark storm of suffering is never the last word. Beyond the pain is a rising sun. Or more accurately, beyond our suffering is the risen Son.
—JAMES EMERY WHITE IN *Life-Defining Moments*

13

Knocked Down a Notch

ose Handford was a forty-nine-year-old bundle of energy and enthusiasm. Everything seemed to blossom under her touch. No wonder that each church her husband had pastored over the last twenty or so years had bloomed right along with Rose and her family. It would be a hard-hearted individual indeed that found something to dislike about this terrific lady. But someone did. Rose was busy fixing dinner, concentrating on pulling a meal together before the mid-week services started at 7:00 P.M. when the telephone interrupted her preparations. Rose answered the call and within five minutes had to pull herself together. She'd never heard anyone, let alone anyone from within her church, use such language and all directed at her. Rose wasn't just shocked, she felt stunned. Then she sat down and replayed the last words this caller had said to her. Those words stung and hurt. Oh why couldn't he have waited until her husband had arrived home?

Rose understood why this man was so upset; still, his offensive accusations were uncalled for and were directed at the wrong person. And then he had hung up on her while she was in midsentence! Rose realized that when it comes to money people can be downright nasty. She had just had the worst experience in dealing with the ruthlessness that cold hard cash can provoke. And to beat all, neither Rose nor her husband had anything to do with the distribution of meager benevolence funds. Heart still pounding, Rose carried on a heated discussion with herself. Should she call this "gentleman" back and set him straight or let him (and her) simmer down before making any attempt to work this problem out? Too upset to think straight, Rose made the most prudent decision possible. She sat down, closed her eyes, and prayed.

"And forgive us our debts, as we also have forgiven our debtors."
—MATTHEW 6:12

Dear Lord, I'm on my knees this time, Lord. I don't think I can recall an incident that has left me so angry before. No one likes being accused of wrongdoing, but by another Christian? It feels unbearable that someone with whom I've shared communion can even think I would be dishonest. Lord, this hurts. I want to defend myself, to prove that this person is mistaken. Yet I believe that right now silence is the best option. Why is it so difficult to be still? I feel this urgent desire to rush over and make things right. I can say one thing, this misunderstanding has taught me that I care too much about what others think of me. I am ashamed to admit this. I never thought I concerned myself with the opinions of others, but I do. This event has crushed me. I know I have to forgive and let it go. You are my judge, not any man.

Yet I want to prove I'm innocent. Even though no one else believes this accusation, I still am determined to turn this around. I really do want an apology. Yes, I understand that this is unlikely. How can I face this person again with vindictive feelings surging through me? It will only be possible as you give me grace. I think of how many times I've counseled others to forgive. Ha! Now, I'm the one needing the admonition. This is much tougher than I realized. Oh, how long will my soul fight against surrender? Help me, Jesus. Extend your abundant grace, your measureless peace to me even this moment. I long to be in close communion with you and that won't occur until I've set this right in my own heart. Right now, give me what I require to relinquish this mess to you. Do as you see fit. Enable me to forgive, to love unconditionally. And remake my hardened heart, I pray. Amen.

It is truly amazing the emotional power that is generated by a group of passionate people sharing their frustrations and anger apart from prayer and repentance.
—DAVE BURCHETT IN *When Bad Christians Happen to Good People*

14
Nimble Fingers

*T*hirteen women sat at an oversized table in the recreation room of one of the group member's house with needle in one hand and thimble in the other. Each lady had two things in common, a love for quilting and a passion for parish ministries. Other than that, these females were more dissimilar than alike, and during some of the quilting gatherings conversation could get a bit dicey. For this reason, Stephanie, the only under-fifty member, had surreptitiously guided each lady to a specified seat, thus minimizing any minor squabbles between the more blunt or verbose of the group. Supposedly, these little frictions occurred in every small town, but Stephanie's heart just couldn't take it. Here they were, the women's auxiliary gathered for the benefit of a yearly auction that divided all its proceeds to three different missionary families—and they themselves struggled to get along. It was amazing. Stephanie also found it demoralizing. She often left these meetings feeling isolated and discouraged. These petty arguments go against everything we're working for, she thought disconsolately. "Why we send missionaries across the world to share Christ's love and we cannot even demonstrate it among ourselves. It's disgraceful and we should be ashamed," Stephanie said aloud.

The remainder of Stephanie's afternoon didn't put her in much better spirits. She kept ruminating over the last few words spoken while the meeting was dispersing. Surely, there wasn't much kindness exhibited today. Almost every lady stopped to check and double-check another's work. It wouldn't do for any stitches to be uneven or lack in uniformity, now would it? Stephanie's stomach churned. "Lord, I'm going to start praying for this group. My first request is that when we meet next week we bring along with our quilting supplies a generous spirit, a friendly word, and an extra dose of encouragement to spread around. Amen."

Applying all diligence, in your faith supply moral excellence, and in your moral excellence, knowledge; and in your knowledge, self-control, and in your self-control, perseverance, and in your perseverance, godliness; and in your godliness, brotherly kindness, and in your brotherly kindness, love.
—2 PETER 1:5–7

Dear Lord, it astounds me that fellow Christians treat each other with more contempt than those of unbelief. How can this be? Within your household of faith you desire unity. We are so lacking in this area, Lord. It grieves my heart to hear how callously we allow ourselves to speak to each other and no wonder, it's an ingrained habit now. The irony of the matter is that we are gathering together to benefit those who are giving their lives for your sake. I believe we are making mockery of their sacrifices as we grumble and complain to one another under the guise of "serving God" with our hands.

Certainly, we can turn this around. Lord, help each of us see that we are commanded to love each other despite our differences. You alone can bridge the gaps that have divided us. Soften our hearts and allow us to see your goodness and glory. Instruct our minds to think according to biblical principles and to then act in accordance with these precepts. Lord, I can only imagine how we have grieved you with our cattiness. Instill in us hearts that are rightly ashamed for this sin. No number of good works can make up for hearts hardened by pride and arrogance. Effect a change in us Lord. Remove the planks that distort our views. I pray that you bring us together again but as changed women—servants who fully grasp your sacrifice, fully embrace your grace, and who are fully determined to walk upon a holy path. Lord, just as you've begun this good work in us, bring it to a beautiful completion. Amen.

> *The cross—that mysteriously and incomprehensible place where man punishes God for nothing, and God punishes Himself for everything. At the cross, man again rejected God's Word, but this time our rejecting Him made it possible for Him to accept us. God ordained His own rejection for our sake.*
> —SUSAN WILKINSON IN *Getting Past Your Past*

I'll Fly to You

*T*rudy was the kind of mother epitomized by the early 1950s television programs. She was everything to everyone. When folks asked Trudy what kind of work she did, she'd just laugh and say, "Oh a little of this and that." More often than not, Trudy never gave anyone a straight answer, probably because she never took herself or her role in life too seriously. She only wanted to be there for whoever needed her. Trudy loved taking care of people, plain and simple. Instead of her kids dragging in unwanted pets to nurse back to health, it was Mom who instigated the temporary hospital they'd set up in the mud room off the kitchen. It was Trudy who would call family meetings to discuss the best way to "get that little girl from down the street to smile more." Although Trudy's loving touch extended far beyond the four walls of their home, she made certain her children and husband were well cared for, too. No day passed without some evidence of Trudy's creative servanthood touching those she loved.

Eventually, Trudy's family grew up and moved away. Each of her three children lived in a different state. Trudy understood that sending her girls to out-of-state colleges would almost certainly mean they'd marry men from out-of-state as well. And they did. Each one in their turn came home for summers and holidays, then all the girls married before saying their final good-byes. It was Taylor, Trudy's youngest and who had only been married four years when disaster struck, who now had Trudy's undivided attention. Taylor's husband moved out of their home leaving her with a six-month-old baby. Taylor was devastated. Trudy, now caring for her own parents around the clock, could no longer drop everything and fly out to be with Taylor. Her own heart was breaking right in rhythm with her daughter's. So Trudy devised a method to stay close to Taylor as well as help her cope with the distance that separated them for now. On the hour, every hour, Trudy closeted herself in her bathroom and picked one bible verse and prayed it for Taylor. Once a day, right after dinner, Trudy called Taylor to help her "pick up the pieces" of the day. Together, though apart, Trudy's determined love found a way to minister to her youngest child.

And in the same way the Spirit also helps our weakness; for we do not know how to pray as we should, but the Spirit Himself intercedes for us with groanings too deep for words; and He who searches the hearts knows what the mind of the Spirit is, because He intercedes for the saints according to the will of God.
—ROMANS 8:26–28

Dear Lord, as always, I come before you so acutely aware that I lack the full understanding of how I should pray for this need. I see only with my short-sighted vision, I don't fully comprehend how you might work this situation for good.

Truthfully, I cannot see how anything good can come from this nightmare. Always, I have been able to lend a hand and assist my loved ones through their troubles. Now I am too far away. There is no simple remedy here for the dramatic pain my dear one is experiencing. Lord, it is almost driving me crazy to think about this person suffering so. Please enable me to think clearly, to pray with purpose, and to continue offering support, ineffective though I think it is. Never let me give up. Help me offer your wisdom, truth that soothes and delivers lasting hope. Show me the words that will be a balm on my loved one's wounded heart. I have nothing to offer you but my praise and worship. Give us your strength, your grace to make it through this horrific situation. Enable her to get up each morning, turning to you for her strength, and give her all that she needs to live. Indeed, give her the reason for living. I pray you might protect her broken heart from hardening, do not allow sin to corrupt her gentle spirit. Keep her in your faithful grip. Amen.

There is great news! Shout for joy! The cross of Christ has bridged the Grand Canyon created by sin, and we never need to be alone again. Nor do we need to try to push through life on our own strength. That is the beauty of understanding God's amazing grace.
—CYNTHIA SPELL HUMBERT IN *Deceived by Shame, Desired by God*

16

Constant State of Emergency

At twenty-nine years old, Liz worked hard to train for her 911 operator's position. After five years of working directly with callers and assisting them to resolve non-emergency situations as well as life-threatening ones, Liz was promoted to shift supervisor. She always felt that she was born for a career such as this. Liz wasn't one to get ruffled or allow her anger to best her. She had long ago developed an inner strategy that helped her cope with the pressures of life—and most certainly in her profession, stress was present around the clock. In fact, it was Liz's calm demeanor that helped tip this supervisory position into her lap. Liz was forced to handle more than her share of emergency calls as she trained fellow staff to do the same. Liz understood that her coworkers had to trust each other implicitly. There couldn't be any guessing games about how one might react in the face of multiple 911 calls, which required everyone's best and most skilled attention. Time and again, Liz's quick decisions made the difference between life and death.

Liz also worked hard to overcome the biases and stigmas that attended being a female interested in moving up in the ranks within her department. Even her friends couldn't understand why Liz would want more responsibility and for not much more pay. But Liz had a gut satisfaction that came only after she'd successfully negotiated a once life-threatening scenario to a positive outcome. Liz thrived on coaching people to give their best in emergency situations. It was a good thing, too. For Liz saw a dramatic increase in domestic abuse cases, teenage drug overdoses, and suicides, along with the normal run of accidents, robberies, and fires. There aren't many like Liz, but for the countless victims who are touched by her care and her expertise, Liz is frequently part of the prayer of thanksgiving offered up by hurting families.

For the Lord gives wisdom;
From His mouth come knowledge and understanding.
He stores up sound wisdom for the upright;
He is a shield to those who walk in integrity,
Guarding the paths of justice,
And He preserves the way of His godly ones.
Then you will discern righteousness and justice.
And equity and every good course.
—PROVERBS 2:6–9

Dear Lord, not many understand my desire to serve my community as I do. They think it strange that a woman can find satisfaction in a place where one sees the very worst of society on an hour-by-hour basis. But I see it in a different light. When I answer a call for help, I kick into action, find a way to solve the problem at hand. Only afterward do I take the time to emotionally work through the difficulties of what has just happened. Somehow, Lord, you've enabled me to think fast, to make decisions quickly. This is what I do best. I admit to loving my career. When I enter my department, I can almost sense an indiscernible change come over me. It's as though I'm pulling on a garment that readies me for service. Thank you for making me so very aware of your presence with me as I labor for my community. I am so grateful that I personally find great satisfaction in my job. It is a rare thing to truly feel blessed as one works!

And now, I call upon your graciousness to supply me with the mental acuity to make the best decisions. Help me to gauge between a good solution and the best solution. Show me how to listen carefully and develop a more finely tuned ability to anticipate potential dangers. Lord, I may have experience, but you alone have the wisdom I require. I am wholly dependent on your insight, your leading as I serve. Take my heart, my mind, my body, and mold me into an effective leader. Use my skills to bring honor to your name. Amen.

He [Jesus] never asks us to give Him what we don't have. But He does demand that we give Him all we do have if we want to be a part of what He wishes to do in the lives of those around us!
—ANNE GRAHAM LOTZ IN *Just Give Me Jesus*

17
ER Overload

It took Tina four tries before she was able to get the IV inserted properly. The poor baby was only nine months old and squirming all over despite his high fever and previous lethargic behavior. Something about needles always sends a shot of adrenaline pumping through both the young and the old, Tina mused. Once this patient's IV was set up and running, Tina moved quickly to the next partition and started taking vitals. She gathered all the information she needed but felt guilty even calling the doctor in to see this particular ER visitor. On another night Tina would have been more patient with a chronic repeat visit to the emergency room—but not tonight. It was a Friday evening, mid-February, and just about half the city seemed to have the same respiratory flu. Tina didn't have the time or the emotional resources to handle a hypochondriac. She placed a large question mark on the chart and left the room.

Not missing a beat, Tina checked on the infant again with the IV, who was finally falling asleep in his mother's arms. This one would be admitted, she guessed. Now to the elderly couple she'd seen a male nurse wheel into the partition on the end. One look at the frail woman told Tina this would be another admittance. A wheezing cough, pale skin, trembling hands, this senior was hurting. Better get the doctor in here pronto. Tina checked vital signs again and promised to be right back. Halfway down the corridor, Tina looked around for the attending physician; she needed to update him on the patients she'd just seen. Strange, Tina thought, he's not in the station, not back with the patients either. Tina took another quick glance around and saw the doctor in question heading her way. With a rueful expression, he explained that a patient had just vomited all over him. He'd needed to clean up and get changed. Tina offered a tentative, empathetic smile and was already explaining what she'd found as they continued walking back toward holding area.

As each one has received a special gift, employ it in serving one another, as good stewards of the manifold grace of God.
—I PETER 4:10

Dear Lord, this is a good profession that I am in. I love the place where you have called me. This combination of skilled care giving is exactly what I've longed to do. I thank you for helping me discover what my unique gifts are so that as I work, I am also using my special abilities to bring service to others. I cannot imagine another career more suited to my personality. Many wonder how I can find fulfillment in my job. They give me such puzzled expressions when I relate what my last shift was like. It is stressful, I admit. Yet I always know that you are with me. I sense your presence, your grace as I go about my tasks. Without your hand steadying mine, I would have quit long ago. But I've learned that as you prepare people to serve you also equip them with everything they need to succeed. I ask that you continue to teach me the skills I must have to deal with frequent emergencies, even frightening scenarios. Help me and my colleagues offer a calm alternative to the hysterics many express when they come in such dire need. Lord, may your peace reign here. I ask that you temper our emotions and enable us to give tender care. And please do not withhold your wisdom. So often we aren't sure what we're dealing with. We sorely need keen insight and intuitiveness to diagnose properly. Give us what we require to assess difficult situations quickly. Help us master our own emotions and work in a manner worthy of our calling. Amen.

The needs of the world and my total ability to minister to those needs decides the worth of my service.
—A. W. TOZER IN *Gems from Tozer*

18

A Fresh Look

orty-year-old Janna was the owner, manager, and head stylist at one of her city's most cutting-edge beauty salons. Having started off working for others and eventually having gone into business while she was still married, Janna had years of hands-on experience working with the public. After her husband left Janna and their two children, it was touch and go for a while. She had had to pull from within herself every ounce of energy, stamina, and stick-to-itiveness she possessed in order to keep her business afloat. But she did it. Although those years were long gone and her daughters were grown and on their own, Janna found herself fighting those weary feelings of exhaustion on a daily basis again. She realized that part and parcel of her career was becoming a master-listener. But over the years, she hadn't realized how much emotional involvement she had with her clients.

From morning until night, Janna was privy to a number of unusual happenings. Whether something worth celebrating, like a new baby or an upcoming wedding, or something tragic and sad, as a terminal illness, Janna was given the inside track. She listened with heartfelt concern. She played intermediary. She counseled and encouraged.

She made contacts between one client and another. All in all, Janna was too involved in the lives of hundreds of men and women. Although she knew withdrawing wasn't the answer, she decided there was only so much of her to go around. Before work, Janna now takes about thirty minutes to leisurely drink her coffee and eat breakfast. She also makes certain she opens her Bible and reads a chapter from Proverbs, the proverbial book of wisdom, to give her what she requires to handle the myriad problems brought to her each day.

"Give me now wisdom and knowledge, that I may go out and come in before this people."
—2 CHRONICLES 1:10A

Dear Lord, you alone bring me to a place of respite and relief and I thank you for that. Daily, I am bombarded with problems too great for me to comprehend. I cannot shoulder the hurt I am privy to each hour. It has become more than I can handle and yet I want to be available to minister to the needs of those who hurt. I truly desire to impart a helping hand or a word of encouragement. Yet I only have so much strength. I realize that I have been trying to carry the load of those who suffer upon myself. I am wearier now than I can ever recall. In all the years of working to serve those who walk through my door, I have never turned anyone away. Now, I am at the edge of a precipice myself, exhaustion has taken root deep within me. Please give me your hand of strength even now. I beg you remake me from my inner heart and replenish my sorely tested faith.

Lord, I need your touch upon my heart today. It is your grace alone that will lift me above the pain and heartache that surrounds me and those I love. Help me to lean upon your strong hand, which enables me to love genuinely yet also protects me. Show me how to achieve that often-elusive position of balance, which Christ demonstrated even as he served the people brought to him. Give me that heavenly perspective that makes sense of the senseless, and renew my hope in the justness of your decisions. With wisdom and kindness, allow me to serve the needy and the careworn. With your goodness, surround me and uphold me. Lord, as you've called me to serve those who come to me, let me be wise and utter only the words that will speak life and hope to them. I am your child. How grateful I am that you surround me with your mighty arms of constant care. Amen.

Wisdom is insight that helps us to make sense of life and its mysteries, complexities, and absurdities. We need wisdom to center us and to remind us of what's essential when life's tensions and unanswered questions are pulling us apart.
—DAVID HAZARD IN *Reducing Stress*

PART THREE

Overcoming Obstacles and Discouragement

*F*riends and family die. Jobs are lost. Illness strikes a child. Marriages crumble. Arguments abound. Workers gossip. Churches split. Money is short. Leisure is nonexistent. Exhaustion sinks deep. All these stresses and pressures are part and parcel of life. How women choose to face these trials will determine how they view life. Is it a suffering marathon of disasters? Or does faith enter into the scenario, transforming even the most tragic loss into something of inestimable value and worth? One life, one opportunity to make a difference.

19

All Undone

*A*t a loss, Cynthia fingered the intricate lace bordering her handmade pillowcase. Its silken threads slid through her fingers. Just like life's energy she thought mournfully. I don't want to get up. What's the point? With Jack gone for the week fishing with the boys it's just me—alone. Tears threatening to spill over again, Cynthia turned to her side and allowed herself a good long cry.

Two years earlier, when Cynthia's youngest son had graduated from college and moved to another city, Cynthia decided she'd had enough of the inside of her rambling house. It was time to take action. Somewhat bored with her slower lifestyle, Cynthia went through training to become a home health care aid. Many of her patients were elderly folk just returning home from a secondary care facility. They just needed someone to help them bathe and get dressed and organized in the mornings. To most people, Cynthia's job seemed tedious, difficult, and backbreaking. But Cynthia loved it. Always having had a strong nurturing instinct, Cynthia relished the time with these older women and men who carried with them a wisdom beyond her own. Cynthia looked forward to getting up and going to her three assigned patients each morning.

Until today. Alone in the house, she couldn't muster the strength to get up and around. Late last night, her favorite client had died. Cynthia's supervisor had called her with the news. All night long, Cynthia had cried bitter tears. And today of all days, Cynthia thought angrily, we were going to dress Marge up and take a photo to send to her granddaughter overseas. She was so looking forward to it. Oh God, Cynthia wept, what's wrong with me? I can't lay around moping every time someone I've met passes away. It was just so sudden, so unexpected. I, the professional, wasn't even prepared for it. Cynthia lay still for a while longer, just thinking of the generous person Marge was. She realized with a start that she could still do something for Marge. A letter, Cynthia thought, I'll write a letter to Marge's granddaughter and I'll do it now.

Sorrow is better than laughter,
For when a face is sad a heart may be happy.
—ECCLESIASTES 7:3

Dear Lord, why is death so very difficult? I can still see the face, hear the voice, and remember the scent of this person I cared for. I pray these memories never fade. I grew to really love this one you took home. I never expected to grieve so mightily for someone I might even have considered a stranger not too long ago. Yet it stings to recall the times we shared. Every memory is bittersweet, Lord. Why is this so?

A part of me wants to linger and reminisce. Another part wants to shut out the memory and walk away resolved not to be hurt again. Lord, I'm in agony here. I want to care for those who need me. But I'm afraid I'm not up to the task of seeing them die. The final goodbye is just too much for me. I want to believe that all I do makes a difference in their lives—that they're not going to get worse, but well. Still, I see their bodies continue to deteriorate and I struggle with facing the truth. Help me offer more than just a warm bath and comfortable care. Show me how to extend myself and truly give my heart. I want to offer them your comfort, your strength. So often, these ill men and women see no purpose in their lives. They want to die. Help me pass on to them a reason for living. Give me ears that will patiently listen to their stories and give me a heart that cries right along with them as they tell me of times that will never be again.

I'm in this business of serving for you, Lord. I want to love each person you bring into my life the same way Christ did. He loved compassionately, gently, and intensely. Lord, give me the boldness to do the same. Let me not hold back when I begin to experience a measure of my friends' suffering. Fill me with your Holy Spirit and empower me to give generously and with abandon. Amen.

Pain puts us all on the run for relief . . . to the refrigerator, the medicine cabinet, the bottle, the mall . . . the list is long.
—BRUCE NYGREN IN *Touching the Shadows*

20

Persistence Pays

Pamela Metz had been promoted to principal of her school district's junior high school just three years earlier. Although Pam had vied for this position, she soon realized that with the increase in pay and prestige came numerous bumps along the road. Her previous position as vice-principal at an elementary school had been a dream job. Her then-boss handled problems with assertive skillfulness. Pam had assumed that in moving up she would deal with her own staff and students in like manner. Yet try as she might, the residual effects of poor supervision left by her predecessor stifled Pam's every creative effort to set a new pace. Some of her colleagues were so stymied by Pam's predecessor's poor management that they refused to deal with Pam fairly.

On one particularly difficult afternoon, Pam was scheduled to meet with the father of one of her students. Though it was an unlikely scenario, Pam hoped that this single dad of four boys would be calmer than the last time they had met. Pam knew and liked this man's son. Sam was not, however, doing well in his classes, a fact that tormented his father, who had never had these problems with Sam's three older brothers. At 3:00 P.M. Pam's secretary announced Sam's dad's arrival. Pam ushered him into her office, closed her door, and then the fireworks started. Within the space of forty-five minutes, Pam, her school, her teachers, even the cafeteria workers had been run up and down the carpet. Everyone, it seemed, was to blame except Sam himself. Although Pam tried to calmly reason with Sam's dad, nothing worked. Without reaching much of a solution, Pam decided to schedule another meeting with several of Sam's instructors and the guidance counselor in tow. Maybe there will be strength in numbers, she thought, exhausted. As Pam sat back down rubbing her eyes, she thought wryly, and all this just because I care about someone else's child.

"Behold, I send you out as sheep in the midst of wolves; therefore be shrewd as serpents, and innocent as doves."
—MATTHEW 10:16

Dear Lord, what a day I've had! Mental and emotional exhaustion just can't describe how drained I feel. I knew going in today that it would be a challenge, and it was as I expected. I'm so grateful I can rip this page of the calendar out and toss it into the garbage. It seems that no matter how hard I try to remain diplomatic, someone takes issue with my ideas. Even worse, I feel as though I'm the enemy. I don't know if I'm made of tough enough fiber to continue in this position. I always thought I would best work in a place where I could make the wisest decisions for the children and their families. I know you've gifted me with leadership and organizational abilities. So why is it that everyone bucks my plans? I do understand that I'm having to undo the messes made by another; still, can't my colleagues see that I'm a different person?

Please Lord, help me get past not being liked. Show me how to look beyond the unkindness, the blame I receive. I need you to minister to my brokenness and uplift my heart. I believe that you alone have placed me here to serve these families. Give me the grace to press ahead despite opposition from a few who make my life miserable. I do believe you are instructing me in the fine art of dealing with unreasonable and prickly people! You have placed me in boot camp for interpersonal relations. Just help me focus on why I'm there. I must see past the bureaucracy and look at the kids I want to encourage. Lord, even tonight, calm my heart and mind. Embrace me in your love and settle my spirit of unrest. I trust that you have called me into this place at this time for good reason. Amen.

May Jesus shatter our corporate deafness. May His brilliance scatter our blindness. May He never be merely first in our lives, but be our very life, our every breath.

—FAWN PARISH IN *It's All About You, Jesus*

21

The Bitter and the Sweet

*E*lisha flipped the pancake as high into the air as she dared. Another foot and the flapjack would have cemented itself onto the ceiling. The kids would have loved it, but Elisha didn't relish the thought of explaining how it got there to her husband. So Elisha restrained herself and settled for more dignified culinary entertainment. No sooner had she served one plateful of steaming pancakes than they were gone again. "Okay guys, watch this," Elisha called across the room. Oohs and aahs were followed up by demands for more demonstrations. "Sorry, no more batter. Finish up your breakfasts while I clean this mess."

As Elisha scurried around with the energy of three women, she was thinking just as fast. Her mind continued to dart from one thought to the next. Preoccupied, Elisha kept waiting for the telephone call. Almost insistently, she scoured her skillet, willing the phone to begin ringing. Elisha was just about finished sweeping up the last vestiges from breakfast with four kids under age six when she heard the shrill ring from the next room. Rushing to answer, Elisha didn't talk long. She hung up the phone, feeling dejected again. For the third time in about eighteen months, Elisha had received similar news. One of her young charges, the little four-year-old boy from next door whom she baby-sat daily, was still sick. His mother, Elisha's dearest friend, assured Elisha she'd call as soon as the test results came back from the lab. Now Elisha felt sick at heart. They were all so hopeful that Joseph's last treatment had done the trick. But there was no cause for celebration today. Elisha's heart was doing flip-flops. We don't want to lose him, Lord. Please heal him, before time runs out. We are desperate for your intercession. Please don't delay.

He heals the brokenhearted,
and binds up their wounds.
—PSALM 147:3

Dear Lord, soon there will be no more hope for this little one of yours. His body won't be able to fight against the disease that's taken hold. Lord, my heart just breaks when I think about how we might lose him. I know that your love is so complete, so perfect, that my shallow affections cannot even compare. I trust that you are going to safely take this loved one into your world. He will be in a place where you've promised that illness, pain, suffering, and tears have no right, no admittance. I thank you for that. I praise you, Lord, for you are the one who has created life. Above all, you have ownership over every created thing.

Still, my heart is frail. I am tempted to argue this case with you. Heal him! Heal his body and let him have his full share of years on this earth. Don't take him from us. But for all my pleading, I cannot know your will in this matter. I only beg for your compassion and your mercy. I ask that you would place yourself in our midst and carry us through this nightmare. Give us the courage to live faithfully day by day. Enrich us with your presence and bestow upon our hearts a vision of what heaven will be. Set our sights beyond the day's pain, the disappointments we face. Lord, let us be your instruments of comfort and care. Help us emulate Christ's tender compassion, and I pray that your Holy Spirit will guide us to all truth. Let us not turn away from you in our pain. Please, do not allow disbelief or bitterness to take root within our hearts. You know how we're struggling to make sense of this tragedy. Help us understand that you are weeping for this child too. Show us your heart, Lord. Lift up our eyes and help us truly see. We are not up to this challenge. Only through you can we continue. Give us what we require to love in both spirit and in truth. Amen.

It's the truth that, when seen through spiritual eyes, a healed heart and transformed life are far more spectacular than a straightened hand or restored sight.

—BILL BRIGHT AND TED DEKKER IN *Blessed Child*

22

For the Best

It was one of the most heart-wrenching decisions Patti would ever make. After three years of nursing her elderly mother in her home, Patti realized with despair that she might not be able to care for her mom any longer. Not safely, that is. Patti's mom had been in the early stages of Alzheimer's when she moved into Patti's lakefront home. Patti and her family catered to Grandma and loved having her with them. With Patti's spacious five-bedroom house, finding the room for her mother was never an issue. But this most recent incident left Patti with knots in her belly. Patti, always on the alert to her mother's good and bad days, was cognizant of her mom's increasing forgetfulness. But her mom had never, ever, left the confines of the house before. Not until last night. Patti assisted her mom in getting ready for bed and checked on her before retiring herself. All was fine. But several hours later, the family dog, Sadie, started yipping wildly. Patti and her husband, Tom, both awoke with a start. Tom looked around the living area and turned on the lights outside the house. Meanwhile, Patti quietly tip-toed to each bedroom and peaked in. Simultaneously, Patti called for Tom and Tom called for Patti. "Come quick," Tom bellowed.

"Oh, no!" Patti yelled, "Mom's gone, she's gone, Tom."

"And I know right where she is. Look out there," he explained pointing toward their cement break wall.

Sitting pretty as you please was Patti's mother. Obviously oblivious to the unusual circumstances of being outside in the dead of night, wearing only her nightgown, and gazing out toward the darkened shore, Patti's mom simply sat. Gulping back the relief, Patti collapsed on the floor, bringing her knees to her chest and just sobbed. She realized that perhaps even love and good intentions weren't always enough in this difficult season of life.

So then do not be foolish, but understand what the will of the Lord is.
—EPHESIANS 5:17

Dear Lord, only you can fully understand what I am experiencing. Did I make a mistake when I invited my loved one to live here with us? Perhaps all my good intentions were misplaced. Didn't I even consider that my lack of experience might bring harm to her? Lord, I love this one more than I can tell. But now, I feel such guilt. Yet I have my own concerns too. Still, I don't believe the time has arrived yet—or am I simply refusing to face the truth? Most days this dear one doesn't remember where she is anymore. Some days she doesn't even know me. Yet I know how to meet her needs better than anyone else. I alone know her habits, her likes and dislikes. I cannot just abandon her to a system—to strangers, no less. Lord, give me your wisdom in this matter. I desire to do right. But I am at a loss. Please instruct my heart and prepare us all for whatever challenges the future may bring. You are my sole provider. I look to you for guidance. Lord, place within my mind what I require to make these difficult choices. Bring good and not harm to me and my family. Answer my heart's cry, I beg you. This matter is urgent and I am so very incapable of handling all that I must do. Please, draw me near to you, comfort me and my family with your constant and reassuring presence. I commit this situation into your loving hands. Amen.

God makes His will known: (1) through His Word . . . as we stop and study it, (2) through circumstances . . . as we look within and sense what He is saying, and (3) through the counsel of others . . . as we listen carefully.
—CHARLES R. SWINDOLL IN *Stress Fractures*

23

This Is Not Goodbye

*C*raning her neck, Marlene tried to maintain eye con tact with the majestic looking line of fir trees as her daughter Jean exited the grounds. It gave Marlene a small measure of comfort to think about her beloved John living here among such beauty. Certainly, meticulous care had been given to both the interior and exterior of this stately nursing home. And Marlene considered how John always placed such high value on the care and keeping of their lovely lawn. Yes, it was a comfort. Still, Marlene held back the tears threatening to spill. Even though Jean brought Marlene over each afternoon to see John, she still felt strong pangs of guilt every day they started on the trip home. Home, what a mightily powerful word that was, Marlene reflected. *I always hoped John and I would live out our days together—not separated by a ten-mile drive. But it wasn't meant to be,* Marlene concluded sadly. *Lord knows I fought this every step of the way. I just couldn't care for John any longer. Even with Jean there to help, neither of us could do for him what he needed. We weren't strong enough, plain and simple.*

Marlene took solace in knowing that John was well taken care of. Fact was, her granddaughter even worked at the nursing home on weekends, so someone on the inside was privy to John's ups and downs. That was a good thing, Marlene admitted.

Yet I still miss him, her heart cried out. He may not know me any more, but I can't help recalling all the good times as well as the bad that we weathered together. Before he got sick this last time, we were more alike than different. I don't suppose anyone wants such a thing to happen, but we have had a good life together. I guess we're both at what some call the jumping off place in life—and heaven is the next stop.

"Blessed are the poor in spirit, for theirs is the kingdom of heaven."
—MATTHEW 5:3

Dear Lord, do you weary of me coming to you with my earthly woes? Lord, I'll admit it, I'm worn out. Tired from the pain, the weariness, the suffering in my body. I'm looking forward to crossing over, to being with you. It's been a long road through this journey called life. I've seen more people hurt, sick, and dying than I have the heart to remember. I'd like to say that through it all, I've never wavered in my faith. But you know better. How often have I come whining about the littlest things? Looking back, I'm ashamed that my faith hasn't grown stronger than it has. For right now, I feel so very vulnerable. It wouldn't take much to push me over the edge into despair. Nothing feels right anymore. Everything seems out of my control, out of my hands. Still, Lord, I need your touch upon my soul. Without your grace to keep going, I'll never finish this race you've set before me. Hold me up, embrace me, Lord. I so want to walk these final years with you close beside me. Show me the way to continue on. Send your Holy Spirit to minister through me. Lord, you're all I have—please don't forsake me now. Turn my heart upward, give me that heavenly vision, that promise of sweet communion with you. I pray that my last days are full of purpose and that I bring with me a delightful fragrance of your love wherever you take me. Amen.

It is a very poor comforter who has never needed comforting.
—CHARLES STANLEY IN *How to Handle Adversity*

24
Call It Grace

*T*ucking her notes back into her leather briefcase, Wendy completed a quick review of the homeless center she was reporting on for her newspaper. It was brought to Wendy's attention that this particular facility was making immense headway against neighborhood crime, juvenile delinquency, and domestic abuse. Although no one could actually prove that this tiny hub of activity nestled right downtown was the impetus for this positive chain of events, all the locals gave testimony to it nonetheless. Wendy, hardened by the years of working with countless "destitute" cases, just couldn't get enthused about this "corner of hope" as the nameless beneficiaries were dubbing it. Still, Wendy was given the assignment and report it she would. Doubtless there was some angle that Wendy would find newsworthy.

Entering through the back entrance used by volunteers and staff alone, Wendy was surprised to see how orderly and well set up the offices were. Although no state-of-the-art electronics graced the desks, everything had obviously been well cared for by the workers. Wendy was greeted with great enthusiasm, and a genuine warmth pervaded each employee's and volunteer's countenance. Taken aback, Wendy had expected just the opposite. She knew how tiresome this kind of labor became as the faithful "do-gooders" heard repeat sob stories day in and day out. But this, this was something magical. Wendy couldn't put her finger on it, but the pulse of the matter was simple indeed. Every person who walked through the front door looking for help received it. What might also have surprised Wendy was that in addition to practical assistance bestowed, every needy man, woman, and child was also matched with a volunteer from one of the local churches who promised to daily pray and intercede on behalf of the person whose name they were given.

At last, it clicked. Wendy finally realized that as grace was extended to these hurting folk, it somehow lifted them up, gave them another chance at a new beginning. And this same grace seemed to return back and enfold the entire community center with its contagious charm.

But He gives a greater grace. Therefore it says, "God is opposed to the proud, but gives grace to the humble."
—JAMES 4:6

Dear Lord, today I learned a new lesson about rendering judgment prior to gaining the facts. I was sorely mistaken about some things. Please forgive my arrogant assumptions. I thought I had seen it all. In truth, I've seen very little. Today that much was made clear to me. At first, I couldn't figure out what exactly I was feeling. Then I got it. You were there today. Your Holy Spirit was inhabiting the people in that place—and that made all the difference in the world. A spirit of love and truth must accompany good deeds. Your grace filled the hearts of those who labored to give hope to the hopeless. It is true. I could see how lives were being changed. I am amazed at how once destitute individuals can summon up the strength to continue fighting their enemies of drink, drugs, and abuse . . . whatever. I thank you for allowing me the privilege of witnessing this transformation. Thank you for opening my eyes. The light did crack through my hardened soul and I finally understood. I would never have believed it had I not been there. I pray that this is only the start of movement of grace that can span our nation. Lord, enlighten and empower your church to step up to the challenge. Show us how your grace changes lives. Beginning from within the walls of our churches sweep us clean. Then let us carry this message of redemption to our world. Amen.

As I seek to look at the world through the lens of grace, I realize that imperfection is the prerequisite for grace. Light only gets in through the cracks.
—PHILIP YANCEY IN *What's So Amazing About Grace*

Cease and Desist

*R*ifling through a stack of college catalogs and scholarship application forms, Karen, veteran counselor, failed to notice the skirmish going on behind her. It wasn't until she heard a resounding thud echo off the metal lockers that she turned around. Immediately, Karen pressed through the burgeoning crowd of rowdy high schoolers and yelled for the two combatants to stop. Too embroiled in their own conflict, neither one of these pumped-up adolescent teens was paying Karen any heed. Karen forced her way closer and attempted to grab the collar of one boy whose own rapid movements were making Karen's attempts comical at best. At last, two male teachers sprinted around the corner and pulled the boys apart.

Thirty minutes later Karen was sitting in the dean's office, along with the school's principal and another guidance counselor. Out of the corner of Karen's eye, she could see both boys, sitting sullen and defiant, with bloodied lips and numerous other scratches and bruises. Karen drew a deep breath, "This is going to be a long afternoon," she muttered. Refocusing on the discussion at hand, Karen, as she had countless times before, had to fight her first instincts to send these two packing. She had had more trouble with the pair since they started in the fall than all the other students combined. Like fire and water, these two kids just didn't mix. Karen listened to the suggestions from her colleagues. On the facts alone she agreed, a ten-day suspension fit the bill. Yet Karen also knew that both boys came from single-parent family homes; their moms worked two jobs just to make ends meet. These weren't "bad" kids, but they did need someone with a firm hand to keep them on the right track. Knowing full well it would mean much more work on her end, Karen asked her coworkers whether they would consider an entirely different mode of discipline, one that didn't alienate the young men but rather got them more involved with other adults. "How about a community service project instead?" Karen queried.

[Love] does not act unbecomingly; it does not seek its own, is not provoked, does not take into account a wrong suffered, does not rejoice in unrighteousness, but rejoices with the truth; bears all things, believes all things, hopes all things, endures all things.

—1 CORINTHIANS 13:5–7

Dear Lord, there were a few moments today when I was ready to give up, throw in the towel, and just plain forget it. I know they're hurting souls. But, oh, how they try my patience. I've spent countless hours trying to make a positive difference in their lives, tried to get them to see how foolish choices will get them nowhere fast. Lord, I need you to extend your wisdom to me. I am about undone here. These struggling youngsters need our understanding and our encouragement. Yet I don't know how to accomplish this task. Nothing so far has worked. Lord, I'll need your strong hand of direction as I attempt to make a difference that will last. Help bring along others who can share this load as well. Put these troubled ones on a right path, lead them to you, Lord. I pray that in your own time you will bring about significant heart changes in their lives and give each one a new start. Lord, you alone can reshape a battered soul, a broken heart. In faith, I ask this great thing for these hurting souls. Open their hearts to see the truth. Show them they are highly valued by you, their creator. Protect them against destructive influences and keep them from continuing to spiral downward. I commit these young people into your care and keeping. Amen.

> *Being a spiritual mentor to your teen doesn't require a perfect relationship. But the relationship must be genuine, caring, and reciprocating. That kind of bond doesn't come with the birth certificate. It requires effort. It's earned.*
> —JOE WHITE AND JIM WEIDMANN IN *Parents' Guide to the Spiritual Mentoring of Teens*

26

The Sweetest Sound

I t was still achingly discordant. Debra winced uncon sciously as her newest pupil tried to play his assigned piece of music. Four weeks running and little Jon still couldn't get the melody right. Debra, renowned as the town's best music teacher, was stumped. Never in her thirty-odd years of piano instruction had she run across anyone quite like Jon. He was an adorable kid. He was always so polite, ready to try anything she requested, and, according to his mother, he practiced a full hour before dinner every evening. Debra was starting to get a tad nervous, since the recital date was fast approaching. She had a lovely evening all planned in their public library, where each of her students could play (and display) all that they had accomplished during the school year. Parents, relatives, neighbors, as well as the library patrons, were invited to join Debra and her students for an evening around the grand piano, followed by a superb appetizer buffet.

Of course, each year Debra had at least one "challenge student" she had to work extra hard with in order to prepare for the recital. But normally, the girls and boys who struggled at the eleventh hour hadn't been dutifully practicing the rest of the year. Not so with Jon. After racking her brain for a way to allow Jon to play without embarrassing himself, Debra decided to offer her students the choice of playing solo or joining her in a duet. It was the perfect solution. "Now Jon can play, and I can sit right beside him to assist," she proclaimed happily out loud. Debra would no longer be haunted by visions of a small, timid boy making awkward plunking sounds on the piano, which echoed abysmally throughout the old library.

When the evening of the recital arrived, Debra was surprisingly calm. She had taken stock and determined that regardless of how Jon performed, they would sink or swim together. As Jon came up front with a sure confidence that shored up even Debra, they positioned themselves on the piano bench. Jon looked up at his teacher and quietly asked Debra if she was ready. "I am now," she confirmed.

And since we have gifts that differ according to the grace given to us, let each exercise them accordingly . . . if service, in his serving; or he who teaches, in his teaching.
—ROMANS 12:6A, 7

Dear Lord, I admit to feeling somewhat apprehensive. I ask that you send your calming presence to surround my young charges and me. I pray that they feel at ease and that you protect their tender hearts from anxiety. Help them concentrate on what they have learned. Shoulder them with your strength and grace.

And, Lord, give me a measure of calmness as well. I sometimes think I take this all too seriously. It's true that my reputation is on the line here as well. As we, my students and I, serve in this manner, I pray that you will be there right alongside of us. Infuse us with your grace and let others see the light of your love ring through the music itself. You are the giver of many gifts, Lord. Let this night of celebration bring honor and glory to you. Let us all worship you in spirit and in truth. Teach us to use our gifts, as learners and as teachers, to bear upon your highest purposes. Show us how to complement one another and bring balance and strength to the body of Christ. Be with us, Lord, endow us with your peace and presence. Let your love shine through our efforts and onto the neediest among us to bring your joy and lasting peace. Amen.

In order to worship, we need to forget ourselves, to lose ourselves in the Presence of God.
—PATRICIA S. KLEIN IN *Worship Without Words*

27

Give Me Five

At the age of six months, Rachel's daughter lost her hearing. But within months of this tragic loss, Rachel wasted no time in trying to figure out how to communicate with her deaf daughter. Still, Rachel was perplexed as to how best to teach Ellie to communicate as she grew and developed. It didn't take long for Rachel to register for a class in sign language. Everywhere Rachel went she was signing. It was a long, difficult transition but Rachel tried to make a game of it. As her daughter grew older, Rachel would look Ellie directly in the eye and sign each time she spoke. She wanted Ellie to become as independent as possible. Looking back, Rachel couldn't imagine life without the gift of signing. Along with learning this vital skill that enabled Rachel to communicate effectively with Ellie, Rachel had been blessed beyond measure in the process. During and after her signing classes, Rachel became acquainted with other families who were struggling to become adept in this silent language of the hands as well. Together they cheered one another on, applauded new accomplishments, and shared each other's disappointments. Each family became like an extended cousin, aunt, or uncle to Rachel. Whenever she hit a rough spot, Rachel would call one of her fellow students and they'd find a way to overcome whatever challenge was facing her. Rachel also discovered the benefit of having nonhearing friends as playmates for Ellie too. While the rest of the family spoke both audibly and in sign language, it was a nice change for Ellie to mix with age mates who signed alone. All in all, once they accepted that Ellie would never again hear, Rachel and her family found ways to open up the world to their beloved daughter.

Answer me when I call, O God of my righteousness!
Thou hast relieved me in my distress;
Be gracious to me and hear my prayer.
—PSALM 4:1

Dear Lord, what words can I say that will fully describe the gratitude I am feeling? I am unable to verbally express how thankful I am that you have done this great work in my heart. You, whom I doubted and was embittered against, turned a tragedy into a triumph. I couldn't understand why my dear one had to lose such a precious capacity. Gone! It grieved and angered me to even think of how difficult life would be for her. Then you somehow tempered my emotions. You helped me work through this pain. Oh Lord, I do praise you. I thank you for your good work done on my behalf. How marvelous that you did this transforming miracle within my heart. I now know that if you had not stepped in I would not have been able to function. The anger I felt would have immobilized me. Thank you again for your great love you have shown toward me.

What joy is brought to me now as I consider how foolishly I fretted and worried over unknown obstacles. You have accomplished so much. Lord, I pray that you continue to guide her as she grows and reveal to her the special work you have designed expressly for her to accomplish. Help her be discerning and use every gift from you. It is you and you alone who have made all the difference in our lives. We thank you and honor you. Continue your work of sanctification in our lives and let us give witness to your faithfulness as we speak words of comfort to those around us. Let our lives and the hardships we have overcome be a beacon of light and hope to others in similar situations. And let all the praise and honor and glory go to you. Amen.

All God's gifts are important. Don't miss out on any of them in your life. After all, you want everything He has for you.
—STORMIE OMARTIAN IN *Lord, I Want to Be Whole*

28
Guilty Relief

Last Wednesday, Kate buried her only granddaughter. For months the family had known that Jenna's condition was deteriorating quickly. Kate was there with her daughter and the rest of the children for the end. It had been heart wrenching to try to explain to Jenna's younger siblings that they must take great care to not hug their sister because it hurt her. Understandably, these little ones were confused and troubled. Grandma Kate took over mothering them while her own daughter managed Jenna's sickroom day and night. Kate was so grateful she was given this opportunity to "do something" to make a difference and help ease this burden.

Together Kate and the kids would plan the meals, shop for groceries, prepare the food, and then take good long walks to the park and back to help use up some of their boundless energy. Kate thought the contrast ironic between her dying Jenna who barely lifted her head from her pillow and the other three children who couldn't contain their enthusiasm for life. Certainly, God was calling sweet Jenna home to him. Kate cried bitter tears throughout the night for the entire family. She wept for her daughter and son-in-law and the loss they would forever feel once Jenna died. She cried for her grandchildren who wouldn't remember their sister in a few years. But most of all, she lamented and prayed desperately that Jenna wouldn't suffer much longer. On the Sunday morning when Jenna did pass from this life, Kate wept again. This time, however, her tears were ones of joy and blessed relief. No more pain, no more anguish, Jenna, her Jenna, was safe now in Jesus' arms. Forever safe. Kate didn't quite understand her emotions though. In part, she felt guilty for feeling such relief. It took time before Kate understood that it is all right to let go when the time comes.

But when this perishable will have put on the imperishable, and this mortal will have put on immortality, then will come about the saying that is written, "Death is swallowed up in victory. O death, where is your victory? O death, where is your sting?"

—1 CORINTHIANS 15:54–55

Dear Lord, today, tomorrow, and for the remainder of my life I will never forget to give thanks for what you have done for my family. I was devastated when my loved one became so ill. Once we knew she wouldn't recover, I thought I would die too. I have never felt such all-encompassing anguish. It took all that I had to get up in the morning to face the next hideous step toward death. Yet all the while I knew that because of Jesus, this tragic illness wouldn't defeat us. I know she still lives. She is safe from harm. No more suffering, no longer is she in pain—and that gives me great comfort. I

*thank you that you sent your son so that we could have life
eternal. I praise you, Lord.*

*Now I ask that you help us who are left behind to cope
with this great loss. Minister to us in our despair. Temper our
sadness with the joy only you can give. Provide the grace we
require to continue loving those left behind. Do not allow the
fear of future loss to hold us back from loving fully those who
are still here. Embrace us when we need you, Lord. Give us a
touch of your love when we experience hopelessness. Step by
step, enable us to grieve and then let go. I pray that your
Holy Spirit will guide us along this path of pain we must
travel for a time. As your spirit surrounds us with your presence, let us grasp how deep your love is for us. Demonstrate to
us our Father's love. I pray that you will continue to walk
this journey with us. Lead us home to your perfect heaven.
Enable us to survive this horror and to set our eyes upon Jesus
who truly is the victor over death. Amen.*

*Wait out the storm. Cry our tears. Do whatever's next. Let people
in to love and help us. Then when the storm subsides, begin to
rebuild.*

—SHARON MARSHALL WITH JEFF JOHNSON IN *Take My Hand*

29

Hide or Seek

*H*elen felt the familiar wave of despair in the pit of her stomach again. As she perused the financial reports listed in her church's yearly report, Helen was sickened. She, for one, did not believe in going further into debt until her church's current obligations were met. The idea of building an impressive sports complex adjacent to their current main offices was indeed exciting. Some families, especially those with children, were pushing this project heavily. Others, like me, Helen thought wryly, believed that any such plan was presumptuous, since the budget was not being met on any consistent basis. I hate to be the one who says no to a plan that will potentially bring in and attract the neighborhood families, Helen voiced internally. But it isn't sound to presume God will provide the funds when our pastors are already having to live on such meager salaries and are taking a cut in health benefits as well. Our first responsibility is to care for our own and do so responsibly.

By now, Helen knew the opposing argument by heart. We have to live by faith, she'd heard countless times during the finance committee meetings. Yet Helen also knew the Bible speaks of wise planning, prudent spending, and contented living. Helen was so weary of fighting this battle. She had taken this three-year position as part of the finance committee only because of her accounting background. Helen understood money. She prayed for God's wisdom in every situation and asked him to make clear the right course. Helen wanted to care for her fellow parishioners' best interests. She knew that one too many overexpenditures would blacken the good name and reputation of her fellowship in the eyes of those outside their faith. There was no simple answer, so Helen continued to pray and commit the entire situation to God once again.

Not that I speak from want; for I have learned to be content in whatever circumstances I am.
—PHILIPPIANS 4:11

Dear Lord, how many times have I come before you in prayer asking you to please take this burden away. I feel like such a Judas. I never really understood why churches could not get along. Now I am beginning to appreciate how intense the struggles get when there are two opposing sides to any issue. Lord, this is not honoring to you. I am so grieved that we are fussing over a potential "plan." What are we thinking? Help me continue to be a peacemaker. Show me how to build bridges between those who have been hurt or slighted. Give us your wisdom to make the best choice in this situation. I admit that I am not contented now. I want to run straight out of the door and get as far away from this conflict as I can. Yet I recognize that you have called me here for this time, perhaps for this purpose. Help me keep my eyes upon you. I desperately need to focus upon the task at hand so as not to allow bitterness or anger to settle in my own heart. It amazes me how despicably we Christians treat one another when we do not agree. Lord, forgive us. Give us your grace to respond kindly and with a generous spirit whatever the decision. Renew our hearts and remake us into the image of Jesus. This whole scenario has spun so far out of control that only you can bring the healing needed to unify our church. I pray that you will give each of us the patience we require to break out of this stalemate to a conclusion. I beg of you to let your spirit reign among us. We do want your will, Lord. Give us the light to see our way. Amen.

Frankly, many of us never want to grow up when it comes to bearing losses. Children cry, whine, blame, manipulate, get angry and throw tantrums, and insist or bully whenever the thing they're denied is even mentioned.

—GRACE KETTERMAN AND DAVID HAZARD IN *When You Can't Say "I Forgive You"*

30
Words of Life

*C*allie looked down at her hand and felt it cramp again. Early stages of arthritis were becoming more noticeable by the week. *Just that much more incentive to get on paper everything I need to say to Jess.* As Callie kept at it, she remembered a few Bible verses she'd memorized way back when in Bible school. Since those years were long gone, Callie made up reminders of those "golden days" with scrapbooks and other memorable keepsakes. In one scrapbook, she had created a book of calligraphy with a variety of inspirational quotes and verses. When she was particularly anxious, Callie would pull out the scrapbook and ponder the words she had inscribed. It never failed to lift her spirits and help her regain a more hopeful outlook.

No one needs a boost of optimism more than my friend Jess does. At this very minute, I can almost see her weeping into her coffee, Callie predicted. She was right. After breaking up and getting back together before a final exit, Jess's husband had made the separation final. Jess had received the divorce papers earlier in the day. Since Callie was the first person Jess had phoned with the bad news, it was now Callie who felt the burden to ease her dear friend's pain. So Callie sat duplicating a scrapbook for Jess. What did Jess call my book? Callie tried to remember. Something about needing that "cure-all" book for herself, I think. Well, by the weekend, I should have a book finished for her and on its way out west. As Callie continued laboring with care, she also prayed for Jess. It was a good thing to meditate on God's promises, which were precious and true. It was an added benefit to come before God with a broken spirit and have Jesus do the mending.

Beloved, I pray that in all respects you may prosper and be in good health, just as your soul prospers.
—3 JOHN 2

Dear Lord, will you draw near my dear friend? She is in great pain and unable to lift herself out of the distress that encircles her now. I would give anything to be with her in person, to wrap my arms around her while she weeps. But this is not possible. So Jesus, help me find creative ways to tell her that I am standing by her through this nightmare. Give me the words I require to bring a smile to her face. Right now she sounds so hopeless. We've been down this road before, and every time you have gently lifted her back to her feet again. I know that you are a God who is patient and full of mercy. I pray you extend your grace to my friend now. She is in such need and is so alone. I can and will continue to pray for her. But she needs more than my simple prayers. Lord, she needs your presence. She must know that you are at her side and holding her up.

When I look back over the years of our friendship, I would never have imagined my friend would have to struggle so. And yet, time and again, she has been cut to the core. I do not understand this. Why is it that some must face one trial after another with no seeming respite? I am not questioning your plan, God. I just want blessed relief for those I love. Please let my friend feel the fresh cooling breeze of joy sweep across her brow today. Let her eyes recognize the beauty still found in the natural world you created and help her take heart in that. Open her ears to hear the words of compassion that loved ones are extending to her, and let them bring her comfort. Lord, above all, give my friend your Holy Spirit as her guide, her counselor, her instructor. I commit my dear one to you, Lord. Take good care of her. Amen.

Faith is belief and trust in God and loyalty to him, even when it doesn't seem logical. It's often challenged when our prayers are not answered in the way we expected.
—JANET HOLM MCHENRY IN *PrayerWalk*

31
Combat Zone

*M*egan routinely shut off the telephone ringer, closed her bedroom door, and even put earplugs in place each and every morning. Right after the kids left for school, her husband went to work, and before she showered and dressed for her own job, Megan did business of a different sort. With a handful of three-by-five-inch index cards of assorted colors, Megan would begin with her first area of prayer—praise and worship. After reading, meditating, and praying these topical scripture verses, Megan would switch to another colored set of cards and another area of prayer— strength for the day. On and on, Megan would thumb through her entire selection of Bible verse prayer cards as she interceded for her spouse, her kids, their schools, her community, and her nation. No problem was too grand or too small for her take time to wrestle over in prayer. Megan realized that praying according to the promises found in the Bible unleashed a power straight from heaven.

Although Megan never saw thunderbolts, she knew she was doing a mighty work, one ordained and commanded by God. This new prayer system also kept Megan's mind on track when she started to think about what to prepare for dinner that day, or how she was going to accomplish everything on her to-do list. Megan was really no different than any other mom on her block. But she knew firsthand that as she invested time in prayer, things changed. Megan also realized that there was no sounder way to show she cared for her family and friends than to sit before God's throne and petition him on their behalf. Not only was Megan having an impact on the lives of people for whom she prayed, God was slowly transforming Megan herself into a woman of quiet calm and great faith.

You also joining in helping us through your prayers, that thanks may be given by many persons on our behalf for the favor bestowed upon us through the prayers of many.
—2 CORINTHIANS 1:11

Dear Lord, I have to bow my head and my heart before you now. I am overcome by a sense of your holiness. You have blessed me. I am amazed at how your love extends to all and knows no limits. Thank you for holding out your hand of grace to me. Your promises are right and true. Amen! I have nothing of value that compares to the love that you have bestowed upon me. Whenever I take these private moments to enter into fellowship with you, I am amazed how quickly you work your way deep within my heart to effect the needed changes. This is such good work that you accomplish in me. And what a rich fellowship we enjoy. I wish I could say it has always been so sweet. But you know the truth. You understand how very difficult it is for me to take the time at the opening of a new day to sit quietly in your presence. How I fight the urge to get up and get going. I am not a contempla-tor by nature. Rather my instincts are to surround myself with busyness and action. Lord, how much I have missed by neglecting our daily retreats. Please forgive my lack of self-discipline. I allow "life" to get between us. And I know that only as I bask in your truth and bring to mind your life-giving promises will I be equipped to handle all that life brings my way. Please continue to woo me back into your presence. You are truly my delight and my only lasting joy. I ask that you never stop using me to bring about miraculous changes for your glory. Keep my heart sensitive to the leading of your Holy Spirit. And help me fix my eyes upon Jesus now and forevermore. Amen.

> *"The former regulation"—the Old Way of getting it right so God would bless—"is set aside." . . . We've been given "a better hope" than the promise of blessings for obedience; we've been invited to "draw near to God"; people like me can now get chummy with God. Amazing!*
> —LARRY CRABB IN *The Pressure's Off*

PART FOUR

Facing Fears

A spouse dies and grief is unquenchable. Terminal illness takes over both mind and body. A child runs away from home and is lost. Growing old alone is almost a certainty. Fears of the future and the unknown are so commonplace. What woman can say she hasn't fretted over what lies around the next bend? Still, for a woman of faith, the unchanging word of God promises every need will be met . . . in the proper time. There is no need for fear or worry or hand-wringing when one's confidence rests securely in the promised provision of God.

Red Alert

Sitting in the waiting room of yet another doctor's office was a commonplace event for fifty-nine-year-old Nancy. She was used to transporting both of her elderly parents to and from their medical appointments. Some days, Nancy teasingly threatened to demand a kickback from the medical group to whom her parents gave so much of their income. Today, however, Nancy wasn't busy filling the time with reading, paying bills, or working on backed-up correspondence. She couldn't concentrate long enough to accomplish anything worthwhile.

Instead of acting as the mediator between patient and doctor on this day, Nancy was the patient. Choked up inside, she was determined not to let her imagination take over. She wouldn't give way to fear. Nancy was also just as set on not getting sick. There was no one else to take over if she became ill. Her parents needed her daily support. Nancy sat grimly awaiting her turn to be called into the inner office. Her mind roiled with thoughts of terminal illness, ugly scars, and gruesome, painful sleepless nights. With a start, Nancy deliberately picked up a news magazine to help take her mind off her fears.

Finally, Nancy thought, as her name was called. After another twenty minutes of impatient fidgeting on the

examination table, Nancy's physician entered the room.
Ten minutes later, a very relieved Nancy left the building
and collapsed in her car. *I need a jolt of something right
now,* she thought wryly. *What if it had been cancer? A
benign lump is one thing, but cancer would have put me
out of commission for months. I'm so glad that's behind
me—us. I don't know what I would have done or could
have done if I had needed surgery. Thank God I don't have
to think about it now.*

---

*Let us therefore draw near with confidence to the throne of
grace, that we may receive mercy and may find grace to help
in time of need.*
—HEBREWS 4:16

*Dear Lord, can I truly trust you, Lord? I want to—more
than anything. I can think of nothing sweeter than laying my
burdens at your feet and picture you sweeping them away
with a single brush of your hand. But too often I feel just the
opposite. I feel like I'm the one who's carrying the weight of
the world on my shoulders. I stumble, I fall. I try to get back
up and I end up sliding down another slope. Lord, I know
that you have promised to never give me more than I can
handle. Your word says that the burden you impose is light.
So why do I feel such weariness? Life is so difficult. Emotions
strain me. I experience far too much pressure. I truly want to
unburden myself and give you my cares. Take them, please.
Then, quickly, before I have the chance to pick them up*

again, will you give me the wisdom to know how to live this life without the excess baggage? Instruct my heart in your ways. Give me the insight and vision to live one day at a time; to leave my future in your so capable hands. I feel desperate for a reprieve, Lord. In truth, I do not know how long I can continue giving away of myself. It would not take much to break me. Even my health is suffering. I try to faithfully meet the needs of my family. I love them! But Lord, I too require assistance. Each day I feel my strength waning a bit more. I don't know the answers. I cannot imagine how you will work. But I am confident of one thing. You are faithful. You will bring together all that I must have to lovingly serve those I care for. Give me your good word of encouragement today. Extend to me your message of peace, and never stop reminding me that you alone are my source of strength. Amen.

God is so unpredictable, so unmanageable, so untamable! But every now and then, He does something that makes me say, "My gosh, You're really there, and my life is in Your hands."
—LARRY CRABB IN *Secrets of a Faith Well Lived*

33

Null and Void

The scuttlebutt had been circulating around the military base for days. But Leslie, part-time military hospital nurse and full-time mom to three children, couldn't get any definite word on where her husband Tim had been sent. It wasn't long before the "where" didn't matter any longer. Tim had been killed on a training mission. "It was an 'unfortunate' tragedy," said Tim's higher-up as he made a public announcement. Although Leslie and Tim had both been in the military since right after high school, they never dreamed that something as innocuous as a training mission would separate them forever. In fact, so confident were they that Leslie and Tim often joked about their unbreakable contract to always come back to each other unharmed. Of course all joking now aside, Leslie, through her tears, recalled small details such as these as she tried to cope with life without Tim.

Staying on at the hospital on base wasn't an option, at least not for another eighteen months, and Leslie was thinking ahead. What should she do after her own term was fulfilled? Leave the military? Sign up again? Move back to her parents' town? She wasn't sure. Leslie recognized how very difficult the next year or so would be just to make good on her commitment to her fellow officers and her children. She was afraid. Unlike her normal, confident self, Leslie was second-guessing just about everything now. It was unnerving how alone she felt, even with the responsibility of her three kids and their constant presence. Perhaps most of all, Leslie felt stunned by the fact that she was facing the rest of her adult life without Tim. Her grief was threatening to pull her under, and she didn't see how to curtail the ever-escalating waves of pain from destroying what little strength she still had left. After a time, Leslie realized she had to do two things: first, call upon her discipline earned through the military to just keep going despite her despair; and second, call on God, the only one with strength enough to handle her pain.

"But as for me, I would seek God,
And I would place my cause before God;
Who does great and unreachable things,
Wonders without number.
He gives rain on the earth
And sends water on the fields.
So that He sets on high those who are lowly,
And those who mourn are lifted to safety."
—JOB 5:8–11

Dear Lord, another morning dawns and I'm still lying here paralyzed with grief. I'm rife with pain. My entire body aches and nothing, nothing eases my sorrow. I never expected to experience such intense suffering. Who could have told me that this is what losing someone you love feels like? No matter what I do, the hurt walks with me. I try to keep busy, get occupied on the day ahead, still my soul is pierced. I'm giving what I've got to my children. But admittedly, it's not much. Like me, they are walking around in a state of shock. But death doesn't leave survivors—only injured, crippled followers. I cannot live the remainder of my days in such a state. I don't want to, and my loved one would want us all to forge ahead and live. Right now, we're not living—we're simply existing. Lord, help us! Give us your hand of strength to press ahead through this nightmare. Bring a new day, a day of hope to our family. I plead with you, Lord, don't abandon us now. We are more in need of your touch of grace, indeed your embrace, than at any other moment. By faith I will get up. I will set a pace for this day. With you by my side, I'll give to my children and comfort them as I am able. But at night, Lord, it all comes crashing back in. The memories, the promises, the future—all dashed. Yet somehow, in that small corner of my soul, I do believe. I hang onto the hope that one day the pain will lessen, another sunny morning will arrive and my first thought won't be one of all that we've lost. Bring that day soon; at least, keep that vision, that hope alive in my heart until I'm ready to receive it. Amen.

Your problems may stay, your circumstances may remain, but you know God is in control. You are focused on His adequacy, not your inadequacy.
—CHARLES STANLEY IN *A Gift of Love*

34

Major Commute

*J*ill fastened her seat belt and within minutes her head was pressed against the headrest in the economy section of the airplane taking her so many miles from her home. Unprepared emotionally for the upcoming reunion with her sister, Ashley, and Ashley's twin sons, Jill tried to relax. No one would ever have called Jill and Ashley close, but they were sisters who cared about one another. The long distance between them necessitated air travel at holidays alone. So when Jill picked up the receiver one evening after work, she was shocked to hear Ashley's request.

Ashley and her two sons were moving back to Jill's hometown. Although Jill welcomed them back warmly, she had not realized at first that Ashley needed her to care for the ten-year-olds for four weeks while she tied up loose ends prior to moving herself. Jill acutely recalled the reasons she was sitting on this very plane. "Jill, I want the boys to get used to their new home and start school at the end of August. I can't swing the house closing and all before mid-September. Can you help me out?"

"Sure thing," Jill had said. Now, some thousands of feet up in the air, Jill wondered how on earth she would swing it. Certainly flying out and visiting for a week before flying home would help her and the boys reacquaint

111

themselves to one another. And there were her folks wait-ing in the wings to pitch in once she got back into town. But Jill knew she couldn't count on her own parents for more than the hour and a half of baby-sitting until she arrived from work to pick up her nephews each day. *What will we do in the evenings? Will they get bored? How will I handle meals, laundry, and everything they'll need? I'm not a mother.* For sure, Jill fretted, *something dreadful will occur while they're under my watch. Oh God, what I wouldn't give for the power to turn this jet around on its tracks.*

Also keep back Thy servant from presumptuous sins;
Let them not rule over me.
—PSALM 19:13A

Dear Lord, I've been called upon to undertake a task that seems too great for me. I am wearing myself out with terrify-ing images of failing those I love. I can't even bring myself to come before you concerning this matter. I'm ashamed that I feel I need to stand upon my own reserves of strength. Why am I embarrassed to admit I may not have all the answers? Something inside me is stubbornly resistant to asking for help. Please forgive my pride and arrogance. I may not reveal it to others, but I am so afraid. I regret that I agreed to care for others' needs when I so frequently botch up my own life. What was I thinking?

There is a part of me that longs to be there for my family. I do want to be of service. So why the hang-ups, the worries, the trembling nerves? Lack of trust in you. At least now I'm being honest. I don't trust that you will help me through this ordeal. Oh Lord, give me a new heart, a brave and stout heart that is courageous enough to say yes. In the inner depths of my soul, I desire to follow your lead wherever it takes me. I want to be called your faithful servant. Still, I don't often get past my own comfort zone. It's too easy to serve under the guise of Christ yet not offer any sacrifice. Please, Lord, reveal yourself to me. Let me worship who you are—my Lord and my God. I long to be more like your son, Jesus, who abandoned all for those around him. Help me take this first and most important step in relinquishing my life for you. Today, this moment, I set down my fears and leave them at your feet. Amen.

And tomorrow, when out of habit you pick your luggage back up, set it down again. Set it down again and again until that sweet day when you find you aren't picking it back up.
—MAX LUCADO IN *Traveling Light*

35
Take Care

Searching the shelves for a travel-size shampoo and conditioner, Amy reconsidered her choices. Maybe this won't be enough for two weeks away and a minimum daily shower, she pondered, especially where Val will be working. She'll be nothing but sweat and grime by midmorning. I think I will get the regular size after all. Marking two more items off her list, Amy glanced at her watch. Whoa, better hurry, almost dinner time. Paying for her purchases, Amy loaded the bags into her van and drove toward home. A vague feeling of regret mingled with apprehension swept over her. Not again, Amy prayed silently. Lord, I don't want to go down that emotional road again. Not tonight. It's our last family meal before Val leaves for the airport tomorrow. I want it to be a wonderful evening. Not one filled with me tearing up every other bite.

Turning her thoughts toward dinner preparations, Amy debated about which vegetable to serve with the juicy steaks she was going to grill. Maybe I'll just toss some veggies on the grill, too. Val likes that best. And she probably won't be eating too nutritiously down south either. Amy grimaced, what am I thinking? I was the one who posed the idea of Val joining up with this missions group in the first place. Now I'm the only one who is nitpicking about what she'll encounter. Lord, help me remain positive. I know this trip will be a growing experience for Val. She loves working with children. She's adventurous and has been interested in missions work for the last couple of years as well. This is so suited to her gifts—but I'm afraid of letting go. She's my oldest child—and only sixteen at that. I never thought I'd be one of those moms who balks when their children venture out. Have I ever been learning some lessons about me! Perhaps I'll be doing some stretching here too.

"But you, be strong and do not lose courage, for there is reward for your work."
—2 CHRONICLES 15:7

Dear Lord, I would welcome a fresh attitude adjustment right now. Somehow I am unable to get past my reservations. I am apprehensive about letting go of my child. But I welcome this opportunity for her! I know that she will learn, stretch, and spread her wings during just such an adventure. This pleases me. Yet my heart is cautious—perhaps too much so. Maybe it's because I've invested so much of myself in my child that I am finding it difficult to release her to the world. I realize that the time is soon coming when she'll leave permanently. This short time away is good preparation, I know. So why does every part of me struggle with the relinquishing? When she leaves, a part of me goes with her. I know that you understand the pangs I am experiencing. You, as God the Father, sent your only son to an angry, sinful world for us. I am tempted to hold her back. I want to tell her, wait a while. But that is not right, she needs to grapple with problems and learn to turn to you for her strength. What better way than in the company of those I trust?

Lord, please infuse me with your grace. Cover my anxieties with your blanket of peace. I place my child, for the countless time, into your care. Demonstrate to her that you are the God who does provide. As she leaves, enable me to say goodbye with strength and confidence, knowing that you are all-powerful, always present, and ready to come to her aid. Thank you for the privilege of coming before your throne with my concerns. I do praise your awesome name. I find renewed vigor for the tasks ahead as I focus upon Jesus. Let me honor you with my attitude and actions this day, Lord. Let your glory shine among all the nations and let it begin here, in my heart. Amen.

If you have committed your life and your child to Jesus Christ, and if you're willing to do your best as a mentor, seeking God daily for guidance and strength, you are adequate for the job. He makes you so.

—JOE WHITE AND JIM WEIDMANN, GENERAL EDITORS OF
Parents' Guide to the Spiritual Mentoring of Teens

36

A Restless Heart

*T*he pilot's voice came over the speaker loud and clear proclaiming the warm and sunny weather that this flight of passengers would soon be experiencing firsthand. But Lynn, a thirty-nine-year-old mother of four, couldn't help but feel torn about this trip. True, she was sitting next to her youngest two children, who were relishing every moment of being in an airplane. It was their first-ever flight and they were in awe the entire four-hour trip. Still, Lynn was thinking of her two older children she'd left behind with her husband. Would they be all right this week? Mentally, Lynn started ticking off everything she'd done to make their "home alone" week more bearable. Lynn had washed every item of laundry, ironed all the clothes, paid the bills, stocked the freezer, and cleaned the house. She'd even passed the girls some extra spending money—just in case.

Regardless, Lynn was a woman who fretted. She worried when she was with her kids and when she wasn't. The Lord had chastised Lynn on countless occasions when she started to allow her mind to be governed by aimless and frequently nameless fears. Although Lynn knew it was wrong to rehash everything that could go wrong, she was almost comforted by doing so. It was like a morbid obsession with her. Lynn admitted that she felt more in control of life when she'd planned and prepared well. But she didn't like to acknowledge the truth that no one is truly in control of life. To admit this meant Lynn would have to do more than give lip service to God. She'd have to relinquish her fears to another, who is far more capable of holding hearth and home together than she. It was a lesson Lynn sorely needed to learn.

⤳

Thy lovingkindness, O Lord, will hold me up.
When my anxious thoughts multiply within me,
Thy consolations delight my soul.
—PSALM 94:18B–19

Dear Lord, I'm almost ashamed to come before you again with this same problem. You know me better than anyone. You alone understand how I struggle against this sin of worry. And I'll name it plainly, for you have called it sin to fret and fear the unknown disasters that may befall me. Indeed, your promises speak of the joys of trusting you. I want to experience that freedom, that pure delight in knowing you and turning to you despite my worries. It is true that I labor to hang onto my fears. I clutch them close lest they overrun me. But despite all my energy to hold tight to these burdens, I cannot do so. Life still will offer me both good and bad. It's only through your gracious and redemptive love that I can ever overcome my fears. I do long to let them go. I know that you have said that when I follow close to you, my burdens are light. So what's the key? How do I set my concerns aside? Is there something I've missed? Just how do I undo the years of habit I've developed as a worrier? It plagues me and it hurts those I love. They don't share my fears and often see me as the one who'll put a stop to plans because of my unfounded concerns. Lord, this has to stop. I want my children to know you as a God who provides and protects. But they won't learn that from me in my present state. Help me unleash my fears and release them into your capable hands. Instruct my heart to keep my mind and my eyes upon Christ. Let me place Jesus before my mind's eye every time I am tempted to fret. It will be a long road to recovery, I ask that you stand with me and stand up for me against my looming fears. In you alone, I will trust. Amen.

> *We can demonstrate a life with God that reflects joy and hope for the present and for the future. . . . This is not a denial of reality, but rather a deep conviction that God is at work and will work on our behalf. That kind of hope is contagious to our children.*
> —JERRY WHITE IN *Making Peace with Reality*

37

Catch Me

Bonnie rolled into her church's parking lot in more ways than one. Using her hands alone, Bonnie could transport herself to and from just about any destination now. Her brand-new van was equipped with all the extras a woman with virtually no leg control required. After an auto accident left Bonnie partially paralyzed from the waist down, she thought her fast-paced lifestyle as she had known it was over. What Bonnie didn't realize was just how vital a role her church family would play in her recovery. For over a year, her fellow parishioners took turns making hospital visits, caring for her dog, watering her plants, and just generally took over managing all the loose ends Bonnie couldn't see to.

When Bonnie was moved from the hospital to a rehab center, her church family moved too. Every day someone came to call. Several of the women took it upon themselves to bring Bonnie her mail, help her work out her insurance problems, and plan for her arrival back home. Bonnie, completely overwhelmed by their generosity, frequently held back the tears as she imagined how alone she would have felt without this tremendous outpouring of support. Always having been a natural nurturer, Bonnie for the first time was on the receiving end of such tender care.

And this attention didn't end once Bonnie arrived home after her house was renovated to accommodate her wheelchair either. One of the college girls needed a home during the school year and Bonnie needed a part-time companion while she adjusted to living on her own again. It was a plan that worked well for both of them. Certainly, Bonnie still struggled. But she was more aware than at any other time in her life that God had indeed created the church body for members to be there to support one another. She was living proof.

And all those who had believed were together, and had all things in common; and they began selling their property and possessions, and were sharing them with all, as anyone might have need.
—ACTS 2:44–45

Dear Lord, how can I ever express how grateful I am for your care for me? I would never have asked for this turn of events. Never would I have believed that my life could be the richer after such a tragedy. Yet it is true. Through this pain you have done a marvelous work within me, Lord. You know my heart. I've always loved to get in and help wherever there was a need. I suppose you gave me the "gift of helps." At least, that is when I feel most fulfilled—getting right into the thick of things and helping straighten them out. Now, it's the reverse. I'm the one who is on the receiving end of others' assistance. I must admit that it has been difficult for me to make that adjustment. How I long to jump up and get busy again. But then I realize that I am exactly where you want me.

I ask that you continue to work within my heart. Continue to embrace me when I'm afraid. My future looks so uncertain. I have to admit that I feel much pressure to plan ahead wisely. Yet how can I doubt your care for me? You have always provided so richly, so abundantly beyond my expectations. I can honestly say that every need has been met and more besides. What a tremendous God you are! You bend down and lift your children up and set them upon firm ground. Never stop reaching down to me, please continue to hold me steady. I need to know that you will always stand with me—especially now that I am unable to stand at all. Lord, I still want to be used by you to help others. Please show me the way, your way. Amen.

Scientists aren't exactly sure how a black piece of carbon is transformed into a dazzling diamond, but they are sure that tremendous heat and pressure are involved.
—BARBARA JOHNSON IN *God's Most Precious Jewels Are Crystallized Tears*

Hers, Mine, and Ours

Leaning hard against the railing of their fishing boat, Trish was trying to bait the hook on her son's fishing pole, but the waves weren't cooperating. "Ouch!" Trish yelped in pain. Blood oozed from her index finger and onto the hook. Jacob reacted with a grimace. "Mom, you're getting blood all over my pole."

"Here, take this to your father," Trish said quite willingly as she relinquished the now blood-spattered pole to her son. What I don't attempt for you young man, she mentally noted. After washing her hands with some antiseptic hand wipes, Trish pulled her sunglasses back over her eyes and settled down to enjoy the ride. How she loved the water. It didn't matter whether she was a passenger on a power boat, ski boat, or a sailboat. Something about cruising over the waves, hearing the splash of water against the boat, and smelling tingly fresh air was very soothing to Trish.

And this Saturday morning, Trish could do with some mental and emotional R and R. It was nine years to the month since Trish and her husband had adopted Jacob. Trish had tried to get pregnant for six very long, exhausting years. Finally, after accepting that her body wasn't going to produce any children, they decided to adopt. Trepidation ran high in those early days of filling out application forms, arranging interviews, and answering personal questions time and again. But once little Jacob was placed in Trish's arms, she knew it had been worth the wait and the struggle. Parenting was everything Trish had hoped for—and so much more. It didn't matter that Trish hadn't given birth to Jacob, he was her son. The only potential upset in the whole adoption scenario had been their semi-open adoption requirements. Jacob's birth mom had requested a meeting with their family. Although they had kept in touch through photos and occasional letters, this would be the first meeting since Jacob was a toddler—and Trish was scared. Jacob knew he was adopted, but Trish was nervous about losing her son's affections. What if Jacob wanted to see his birth mother more and more? Was she opening a can of worms here? It didn't matter what she felt, Trish had already agreed. It's just another season of parenting I'll have to face head-on, she thought grimly.

Devote yourselves to prayer, keeping alert in it with an attitude of thanksgiving.
—COLOSSIANS 4:2

Dear Lord, it's a puzzling thing that moms can take what is the greatest of life's blessings and somehow twist it into a worrisome nightmare. Parenting our children, little ones given us by you, is a woman's greatest privilege on earth. Yet I am continually tempted to fret and stew over circumstances beyond my control. At each and every turn, I've prayed and you have answered. Why then am I so afraid at this new juncture? Perhaps I love my child more each day and the thought that his affections might transfer to another haunts me. The tender love we share is such a miracle to me. It astounds me that families can experience such camaraderie. I don't want to let anyone else in. It scares me to think of jeopardizing my child's love.

Lord, minister to each of us, give us your grace to press forward and to love one another from a pure heart. Take away the anxiety, the apprehension. Replace my troubled heart with a heart of peace. Lord, even in this situation, I seek to bring honor to your name. Amen.

I force my mind off problems concerning my children and let my thoughts rise to the throne room in heaven where the four living beings continually worship the Father singing, "Holy, holy, holy . . ."
—JEANNIE ST. JOHN TAYLOR IN *How to Be a Praying Mom*

39
When I'm Gone

*P*ushing seventy, Amanda was as energetic as any fifty-year-old she knew. Amanda had always kept busy either with work around the house, volunteering at various community centers, or helping her daughter Jayne reach her fullest potential. At forty-nine, Jayne's accomplishments were numerous. She had completed her high school education, worked at several grocery stores, served in their church's infant nursery, and was now employed at a local nursery caring for plants and flowers. Jayne, most definitely, was well received wherever she went. Although mentally slow, Jayne wouldn't be labeled mentally disabled, whatever that innocuous term meant. Still, Jayne would never live on her own. She would always need a companion to help her.

As the years passed, Amanda became more and more concerned about her daughter's future. Questions arose in Amanda's mind that wouldn't be quelled. When she died, exactly what would happen to Jayne? There were no siblings, no close cousins, and no living relatives at all who could step in and take over. Albeit unwillingly, Amanda started researching any nearby assisted living facilities that might work well for Jayne. Although she hated the thought of tearing Jayne away from the family home and the garden Jayne so loved, it may be their best option. Praying for another direction, Amanda had a brainstorm. She'd ask the women who served with her in teaching foreign ladies to speak English for some suggestions. There were a total of eight local women who volunteered every Monday afternoon to come in and teach for two hours. Surely one of them would have some ideas; maybe this would provide Amanda with some fresh resources. Exhilarated at the thought, Amanda called Jayne and told her to put the casserole back in the refrigerator, they'd be going out for dinner tonight.

"I am the good shepherd; and I know My own, and My own know Me, even as the Father knows Me and I know the Father and I lay down My life for the sheep."
—JOHN 10:14–15

Dear Lord, thank you for giving me a renewed boost of hope, Lord. I truly needed to know that you were hearing my cries for help. All these long years, I've prayed for my child. I've asked you to show me how I'll care for her after I'm gone. No answer has ever come. In truth, it still may not arrive, not yet. But inside my heart I am confident of one thing. I am sure, beyond any doubt, that you will step in and care for her when something happens to me. I thank you for reassuring my weak faith. You are truly the father to the fatherless and the widows. Can I count the times when you have brought the right person to help us? Is there any way I can express how confident I am in your continued love and support toward us? No, short and simple. There is no adequate way to express my gratitude. At this moment, my heart is over-flowing with relief. Blessed, joyous relief now consumes me. Thank you for your abiding presence, your touch of grace, and your boundless love.

As the years progress, I ask only one thing. That you continue to keep my child and me on track with your will for our lives. Build a hedge of protection around us both. Temper our desires, squelch our fears, and bestow upon us your matchless strength. Give us, day by day, what we require to grow into the women of faith you desire us to be. Set the stage, Lord, for a solid future, one filled with a steadfast con-fidence that you will provide. Let contentment and peace rule in our home. Instruct our hearts in your ways from morning until evening, and teach us how to walk in the light of your love. Amen.

I saw him [Jesus] come again and again to the destroyed souls around me, and the certainty of his love changed the battlefields of my life to playgrounds of joy. . . . Now I fearlessly believe two things: in his love anything is possible and all things are certain.
—CALVIN MILLER IN *Jesus Loves Me*

40

A Little Bundle of Surprise

Susan's jaw clenched, her hands on the handles of her bike in a death grip as she rode like the wind. Another twenty minutes saw Susan still pressing against the March gale, extending everything she had to keep going. About midway home, Susan started to relax some—not from any internal release but from complete exhaustion. She rode until her legs felt like jelly and her forearms ached. Her temples throbbing, Susan gingerly got off her bike and put it in the garage. Once inside her kitchen, she collapsed onto the oak bench and sobbed. Great heaving cries poured from Susan's heart. This just couldn't be happening, she lamented. It can't be true. I'm almost forty-six years old and I'm pregnant? Why now, Lord? Why me? After all those years of trying to have a baby and it never happened? All those failed attempts to adopt? Finally, Dave and I accepted the hard truth that we wouldn't be having any children of our own. Now this? It makes no sense to me at all, none whatsoever. I'm not happy with this. This must be some kind of strange dream, an ironic twist of my otherwise fairly normal life.

Wiping her eyes, Susan's internal tirade abated a bit. Then the tears started to flow again. With a now pounding headache, Susan started to reach for the aspirin bottle, then put it back. Instead she filled her ice-pack, grabbed a blanket, and headed for the couch. Laying there, she closed her eyes and just balled. All those dreams from years earlier came flooding back full force. She was reliving the pain of every single disappointment. Now Susan didn't know what to feel. Upset? Shocked? Elated? Angry? Afraid? Thrilled beyond words? . . . This scenario no longer fit with Susan's plans for her life. Taking a deep breath, she decided to try to stop thinking about it and just rest . . . until Dave came home from work.

Every good thing bestowed and every perfect gift is from above, coming down from the Father of lights, with whom there is no variation, or shifting shadow.
—JAMES 1:17

Dear Lord, this morning I had no clue as to how my life would change before the day's end. I continue to ask myself how can this be? How did this miraculous thing occur? Lord, I am not pleased with the news. This is too much to comprehend. How can it be? I cannot stop asking that question. My emotions are running from one end of the spectrum to the other. I don't know how to deal with the jumble of feelings and thoughts that are all pressing for attention in my mind. This changes everything. We will have to reexamine our lives, our plans, and our dreams. Help me, Lord. Show me how to cope with this news. Help me level out emotionally so that I can think properly. I'm falling under my own rush of emotions. No one can understand what this means to me. Many years ago, I laid to rest my dream. Now you are returning it to me and I'm afraid. I don't want to open my heart's door even a sliver. I really do fear it will come slamming shut again. I am trying to trust in your sovereign plan for my life. But I'm not succeeding too well at the moment. Please help me make sense of this situation. Give me your wisdom. Show me how to cope with this new development and to do so in a way that honors you. I know that you only give your children good things. I pray that you prepare us as we meet the challenge together. Knowing you're with me comforts me exceedingly. Amen.

> *Put the past to rest; look forward; dream big dreams; go for the gold. Run to win, even when the chains are clanking along behind you.*
> —JEAN LUSH WITH PAM VREDEVELT IN *Women and Stress*

41

Be Still, My Anxious Heart

*T*apping her pencil in nervous repetition, Peggy didn't realize what she was doing until her coworker, Alice, frowned in her direction. Sorry, Peggy mouthed. But before Peggy knew it, she was tapping again. Another frown, and she clasped her hands together. Keeping her ears in tune for the tiny *bing* that sounded whenever she received new e-mail, Peggy reluctantly went back to composing the financial report letter for their steering committee's meeting later in the day. "I've got to get this finished," Peggy whispered to herself. Looking back at Alice, Peggy wondered how long she'd been sitting there aimlessly tapping her pencil before Alice motioned to her. I've never experienced a morning that dragged by like this one before.

No surprises there, Peggy thought to herself resignedly. Peggy's god-daughter, Marie, had just sent a lengthy e-mail last evening. As Peggy read its contents she was thrilled how much progress Marie's missions team was having with the refugee children they were helping nurse back to health. Marie couldn't contain her enthusiasm, and Peggy rejoiced right along with Marie. This two-year stint in South

America was the perfect fit for Marie with her nursing skills and her obsessive love for kids—any kids. Peggy tried to will back those feelings of exuberance she'd experienced last night but couldn't. Ever since Marie's mother had sent an urgent e-mail message earlier in the day calling all Marie's family and friends to pray for her safety, Peggy was nothing but distracted. More of a doer than a contemplative type, Peggy struggled to stay at her desk. Yet there was nothing she could "do" at the moment—except pray. As she typed, Peggy rattled off a dozen or so short, to-the-point entreaties to God. "I care for this girl like she was my own, Lord, protect her now. Place your angels on guard around her. Amen."

"My Father, who has given them to Me, is greater than all; and no one is able to snatch them out of the Father's hand."
—JOHN 10:29

Dear Lord, you are my only hope and source of strength. In this situation, where I am so very far removed from someone I love, someone who is in danger, you alone can offer protection. Lord, go now, I beg. Send your legion of angels to encircle this loved one of mine. Show her your mercy and your grace. I ask you to give her your complete and abiding peace, as she must be strong for the sake of those under her charge. Beyond anything else, I wish I could be with her now. Instead I am left here to stand guard, to stand in the gap and offer my requests to heaven. I am so thankful that Jesus sits at the right hand of the throne always interceding for us . . . for her. Please, Lord, even now hear my prayers. Bring a righteous end to this terrible ordeal. Let not darkness have victory. Bring light to this evil place and overcome it with your love and holiness. Endow each person who is there with your strength and resilience. Show them your glory and your willingness to lead them. Give my loved one all that she requires to offer comfort to those who are afraid. Help her recall all the faithfulness you have extended to her in the past. Let her memory be filled with the great and wonderful ways you have provided for her every need. Still her restless heart and allow her to rest peacefully within her soul. Bless her, Lord. Cover her with your almighty hand of protection. Let not any harm come to this, your dear one. Let your name be lifted high. Lord, let it be so even now. Amen.

God does not require polished theology or flawless faith in prayer. But God may well require a total outpouring of body, mind and soul in prayer as the act of loving him with our body, mind and soul.

—DAVID HANSEN IN *Long Wandering Prayer*

PART FIVE

Discovering Joy and Satisfaction

*U*nderstand that many of life's most difficult trials eventually run full circle and at that point come joy, completeness, maturity, contentedness, peace, and a sense of fulfillment. The key is finding a way to see beyond the temporal ugliness and find a path through the pain. Only God's constancy and care can ensure a safe trip through life's many minefields. Take him at his word and embrace his offer of power, love, and soundness of mind. Every woman needs these precious resources for the journey. What's so wondrous is that these gifts are available, without measure, simply for the asking.

Sacred Chore

Positioning the multicolored tulips just so, Sara spoke tenderly to the blooms as though they were alive. Her mother's graveside still brought Sara some inner tranquility and peace. This poignant tribute to her mother's wonderful life was a place Sara came back to on a monthly basis. Sara always brought the most vibrant colored flowers she could find because they reminded her of her mom's sparkle and love for living. Once Sara arranged her tulips to her liking, she knelt down and pulled a few stray weeds and reread her mom's tombstone engraving. It made her smile. Everyone who knew Sara's mom immediately recognized her as a kindred spirit. She always brought out the best in people—friends as well as strangers. Although it used to embarrass Sara to no end when her mother would strike up conversations with sales clerks, delivery people, and waitresses, Sara knew each person felt better after conversing with her mom. Some called it the gift of gab. But Sara recognized it as so much more. Not just an ability to talk. No, her mom engaged people's hearts and inspired them. "No wonder you're so missed, Mom," Sara whispered.

Sara drew herself up and brushed off her knees. She looked around the cemetery and suddenly felt careworn. It usually happened this way. Sara would recall the good times and then just when she was ready to say goodbye, she'd reminisce about the moment some twelve months' earlier when she'd said the last farewells to her mom. As Sara knelt over her mom's bedside, she couldn't stop the tears from cascading down her cheeks. She knew how much pain her mom had been in. Cancer of the stomach had wasted her mother away into a wisp of a woman. Her last memories of her mother were painful indeed to recall. Still, Sara mused, cancer and all its ravaging forces never stole her sense of humor or her zest. Sara, emotions now full circle, was ready to go. "Bye, Mom. Love you."

The memory of the righteous is blessed.
—PROVERBS 10:7

Dear Lord, thank you for giving me such a wonderful example of walking, talking, breathing love in my life. I cannot imagine another who would have inspired me to live life with the courage, hope, and conviction that my dear one did. I admit that I miss her terribly. Yet her legacy to me is so strong, so alive still that not a day passes when I don't recognize her hand of care upon it. There are times when my first thoughts of the day are to call her and burst out with some crazy new scheme. Then I remember she's gone and an emptiness surges through me that is indescribable. I can never turn back the hands of time and I regret the loss. Even though I know she is with you, pain-free in Christ's presence, I still sometimes would call her back. I need her influence and her outlook. Lord, help me remember all I learned from watch-

ing her. Give me the right words to bring blessing to those I encounter, just as she did. It would be such a legacy if I could carry on in her stead. Though that seems daunting, I know you allowed her influence to mold me. Show me how to love as generously and with her abandon. Teach me that I can press ahead and demonstrate that same compassion toward others as she did so lavishly. I am reminded that this life is frequently filled with pain and struggle. Yet you've called us all to join together and serve in every way we can. You've equipped each of us with the gift to lift burdens. Never allow me to forget what I've learned. My loved one invested her very life in the lives of others. Make me willing to do the same. Amen.

If we're open to it, God can use even the smallest thing to change our lives . . . to change us. It might be a laughing child, car brakes that need fixing, a sale on pot roast, a cloudless sky . . . or even a pair of shoes.
—DONNA VANLIERE IN *The Christmas Shoes*

43
Sitting Pretty

To the day, Darlene and Douglas had been together forty-nine years. On this their anniversary, they decided to celebrate their long and happy marriage with an early evening meal set in their garden gazebo. Both of them were avid gardeners, and nothing would be finer than to enjoy a leisurely dinner outside where they were surrounded by their beloved flowers. Darlene planned the menu carefully and decided to order Douglas's favorite dessert from a nearby bakery. She'd chill the shrimp and he would grill the tender filets. As Darlene finished rinsing lettuce for their salad, she regarded the empty crystal vase sitting on the dining room table. Why not, she thought. Today's a day for bringing out the best of everything.

Cleaning up the salad mixings, Darlene carefully placed the salad plates back into the refrigerator and called out to Douglas. Once she had dispatched him to pick up their dessert, Darlene grabbed her garden scissors and went outside to cut the most luscious roses she could find for their anniversary centerpiece. Kneeling down, Darlene cut several vibrant yellow flowers and was deciding on her next selection when she felt it. Oh my, that hurt. "My knee again," Darlene moaned. Ouch! Trying to place pressure on her right knee was going to be tricky. And wouldn't you know it? thought Darlene ruefully, I didn't bring my cane out with me. Gingerly settling back down front and center of her delightful roses bushes, Darlene giggled and winced. Well, at least the sun is shining and Douglas will be back shortly. I suppose I'll just begin my own personal anniversary celebration in private for a bit, she mused. Eyes wide open, Darlene looked up toward the sky and prayed, "Lord, let me say again how very grateful I am for this life you've given me. It hasn't been all roses and fine dinners . . . but you've taken pain and heartache and transformed them time and again into something beautiful. Thank you, Lord, you continue to amaze me with your goodness."

Two are better than one because they have a good return for their labor.
For if either of them falls, the one will lift up his companion.
—ECCLESIASTES 4:9–10A

Dear Lord, what a good and gracious God you are! I have so many blessings for which to be thankful. Not the least of which is my beloved family. Certainly, there have been snags in the road. Still, I would not trade my lot for any other. You knew what you were doing placing us together, and I thank you for it. Even now, you have given us the gift of companionship. We have seen so many lose their way in the midst of suffering and sorrows. Yet by your grace, you have hemmed us in and cared for our every need. I give you thanks from the depths of my heart, Lord. You alone are truly worthy of praise. All around me, I see your marvelous handiwork in creation. How honored we are to share in this beauty. Continue to give us eyes that recognize your hand of care on our lives. As we grow weaker, bestow upon us your strength. Give us courage to face the future, even though certainly one day we will face it without one another. As we live these golden days, Lord, keep us faithful, grateful, and content. And please remind us daily how you are always close by at hand whenever we need a lift. No matter how dark our coming days may feel, continue prompting us to look heavenward. Keep our hearts and minds on the promise of heaven and of being in your presence evermore. This day, let us rejoice and be glad. Amen.

> *As we draw near to Him, children thirsting for His love, He will admit us to His secret place—a special residence of refuge and protection, of revelations concerning His ways and His character.*
> —CYNTHIA HEALD IN *In the Secret Place of the Most High*

44

Doing the Heart Good

etty and her husband, Carl, were enjoying a rare night out alone. No kids and no phone, cell or otherwise, meant no distractions. Well, almost no distractions. While Betty was relishing the fact that tonight meant freedom from cooking duty for her, she couldn't tear her eyes away from the charming scene being played out at the next table. Sitting in this quaint family-style restaurant sat a youngish mom and a nine-month-old boy who was smiling at all the nearby patrons to beat the band. Directly across from this mom sat an elderly gentleman, proud as could be to be sitting in the presence of his granddaughter, perhaps, and his great-grandson.

Betty and Carl conversed together about their upcoming plans for the weekend. Together they ate, relaxed, and just unwound as only long-married couples are wont to do. But Betty's gaze continued to stray over to her right. She couldn't help being captivated by this unlikely scenario. A young mom patiently spooning food into her son's eager lips. Then without missing a beat she'd pull her chair back and lean over to assist her elderly companion with cutting his food. Betty looked at the fresh face of this woman and marveled how composed and completely relaxed she seemed. What a treasure she must be to her family, Betty admired.

All too soon, Carl had finished his dinner and Betty drank her final sip of coffee. They would leave momentarily. As Carl paid the bill, Betty noticed that her neighboring diners were leaving too. This caring mom fitted her son into a snowsuit and then helped her grandfather into his coat. Together the three of them smiled at each other, surely relishing every moment of their treat. Betty had a sudden urge to follow them outside, to thank these strangers, but she didn't. It was enough, what she'd just seen for the last hour or so, to give her a renewed sense of service toward her brood.

With good will render service, as to the Lord, and not to men.
—EPHESIANS 6:7

Dear Lord, thank you for the blessed reprieve you offered me. I cannot express how grateful I am to have the quiet time away. It did my heart good. Lord, I am in awe of what your abundant love can inspire. For surely it is your love alone that sets in motion such unselfishness and service. As I sat contemplating my life, I felt the tears sting my eyes. I was reminded how impatient and neglectful I am with my own dear family. Far too often, I feel not love, but resentment. This is wrong. It grieves even my hardened soul. Lord, was this evening meant to tenderize me? I pray it is so. Remake this tough heart into a caring one that loves and serves and gives without end.

In Jesus, you have offered us the most remarkable example to emulate. Yet for all our admiration and devotion, we don't follow in Christ's footsteps. We are so busy with our own private agendas—far too distracted to listen to the needs of those around us. I could very well call myself Martha yet I long to be a Mary, the one who so wisely chose to sit at Jesus' feet and drink in all that he spoke. Life-giving words were what Christ offered while he walked on earth. Let me continue to go to the well of your promises and drink afresh. Lord, instill in me an insatiable desire to break free from the bonds of my own constraints. Free me to serve you and your people with love that knows no end of sacrifice. Amen.

Grace is a risky business. If we understand it, if we embrace it, we will never be the same. I have heard it defined like this: Grace declares us worthy before we become worthy.
—SHEILA WALSH IN *A Love So Big*

45
Touch Point

Kim raced home from her job, weaving in and out of traffic as boldly as she dared. Kim had even turned down two last-minute appointments at the beauty salon where she worked in order to make it home in time. Although she needed the extra cash, Kim realized that tonight was important, and the little bit she'd make doing a few more cuts wouldn't compare. Rush, rush, rush, it's all I do these days, she lamented. A quick side-trip into her nearby grocers and ten minutes later Kim was again speeding down the two-lane highway to her turn-off. After thirty minutes of pressing pedal to the metal, Kim felt spent. Once inside her condo, she offered a brief greeting to her cat Midas before changing into sweats and reentering her kitchen.

Now, completely undone, Kim grabbed her cherished, dog-eared cookbook and thumbed through until she located the soup section. A chunky clam chowder was on the menu, along with broiled chicken breasts, fresh asparagus, and French bread for dipping in oil and Parmesan cheese. Dessert, the reason Kim had made one final stop en route home, was a selection of flaky pastries her brother Greg was so fond of. Preparing the ingredients for her chowder, Kim began to unwind. She allowed herself the pleasure of smelling each ingredient as she added it to the mix. Mmmmm . . . smells so good. By the time she'd got the soup simmering, Kim's emotions started to stir as well. She felt the satisfaction that only arises after putting some real creative effort into making someone else feel loved. Perfect, Kim said mentally, everything will be just perfect. Greg will be so surprised that I've remembered all his favorite foods—and all to celebrate his last day of exams! This is going to be fun. I can hardly wait to see the look on his face. It's been far too long since this brother of mine and I have spent an evening together just catching up.

So then, while we have opportunity, let us do good to all men, and especially to those who are of the household of the faith.
—GALATIANS 6:10

Dear Lord, what a blessing it is for me to have the opportunity and the means to share good things with someone I love. I don't often take the time to give as I should. It seems that time itself is against me in this. I want to give, to give graciously, and to give often. But I get so distracted by the commitments I've made and then I forget. My good intentions frequently become just that: intentions. Help me set aside time to serve those around me—to spend quality and quantity time with the people I love. It's a wonderful thing to be at peace with one's family and to enjoy warm relationships with those around us. I never want to neglect them. Show me just how important it is to work at staying close to others and to making time to be together. My schedule, my work, even my church responsibilities all press in and edge out my time and energies. I want to make a new commitment to work diligently to spend consistent time with my family and friends. Give me creative ways to express my love for each of them. Place in my heart a renewed desire to show them how much they mean to me and to you. Lord, give me the wisdom to say no to the nonessentials so that I have the freedom to embrace the most important. Beyond my career and my accomplishments lie the real jewels of a successful life. And it all revolves around people. People you love, people who are hurting and anxious. Day by day, please allow me to offer you a set of willing hands and feet to go where you send me and love. Lord, let me be your ambassador of gentle care to these tender souls. I want to serve them in your name and for Jesus' sake. Amen.

The initial burst of spiritual flame may be more dazzling, but the heartfire's greatest effectiveness occurs as it burns into consistency.
—DONALD S. WHITNEY IN *Ten Questions to Diagnose Your Spiritual Health*

46

Kindred Spirits

*C*assie turned twenty-four years old on Saturday. Today, the following Sunday afternoon, Cassie was getting married. All told, Cassie was already figuratively walking in the heavenly realms, so delighted was she to be marrying. She and Jim had waited over four years before this blessed day arrived. With her finishing up nursing school and Jim completing his master's degree in education, both of them agreed that the time passed more quickly than they had expected. Still, Cassie held one regret on this the most treasured day of her life thus far. Cassie's heart lurched when she considered how infrequently she would see her sister Corey. Always, it had been Cassie and Corey. No matter that Corey's trauma at birth had left her with a disabling case of cerebral palsy. Even though Corey couldn't keep up with her older sister Cassie in outdoor events, they were closer than best friends; these two young woman were kindred hearts. Unlike most siblings, the girls exhibited a rare and unselfish love that evidenced itself on a moment-by-moment basis.

As Cassie once again faced the hard truth that she would be moving across country in just a few weeks, the tears spilled. Trying hard to regain control of her emotions, Cassie turned her attention to Corey's birthday gift to her.

A birdhouse! Corey had researched what type of birds inhabited Cassie's new home and purchased a birdhouse, feed, and a birdwatching manual—with binoculars to boot! That same afternoon, Corey asked her father to place her own brand new birdhouse right outside her bedroom window. "Together, each morning, we'll be able to look outside and listen to the birds chirping away . . . it's something that will remind us of each other," Corey had written in her birthday greeting to Cassie. Spying the ten-pound bag of bird seed leaning against the wall, Cassie smiled. *Always the one to lift me up,* Cassie thought with tenderness. *Even though we're apart, Corey's found a way to keep us together. We'll never be far apart though many miles lie between us.*

And do not neglect doing good and sharing; for with such sacrifices God is pleased.
—HEBREWS 13:16

Dear Lord, how does one say goodbye to the person closer than anyone else on earth? I find it difficult to even contemplate my future without my beloved friend. I cannot remember a time when we weren't together, laughing, sharing, conspiring. It hurts my heart to think about planning my days without first conferring with her. It's not that we cannot exist without each other. But from the very first you bonded us together.

Lord, I need your perspective at this time. I am so desperate for your strong hand of guidance and confidence to hold me firm. As I enter a brand new phase of life, I ask that you take my hand and instruct me on this unknown path. I desire to bring honor to your name no matter where I live. I also ask that you take special care of my loved one. Love her and bring into her life all that she needs. Provide her with the friends she'll require and renew a sense of purpose in her heart. This leaving will mean adjustments all around. But I am confident that you will orchestrate the details so that each of us is so very aware of your continued presence, and your promises to work for the good will be evident. I commit this day to you now. And I thank you again for all the blessings a loving family brings into a life. Amen.

Friendship marks God's method for getting things done.
—MICHAEL W. SMITH IN *I Will Be Your Friend*

47
Your Hand, Please

Doris bent over the frail form in front of her. She gently grasped Lily's wrist and turned it over while she positioned the blood pressure cuff around Lily's upper arm. Dear Lily never even stirred. How Doris hated these 2:00 A.M. checks on her elderly patients. More than anyone, they needed the little sleep they were able to get, and having to take their vital signs every four hours around the clock sometimes made no sense whatsoever to Doris. The poor woman's already hooked up to countless monitors, why wake her needlessly? Still, protocol had to be followed, so Doris dutifully made her rounds.

While Doris worked her way down the ward of this private care facility, a step down from a major hospital but more than just a nursing home, she considered each person who slept, or tried to, in these quaint rooms. Everyone has a story, Doris's eyes crinkled with remembered pleasure. I'm one of the privileged few to be privy to all their past histories, their secrets, and their successes. Whoever said that working with the elderly was a no-win situation? Well, they were wrong. I've been treated to tales that had me roaring in laughter, given the sweetest hugs imaginable, and even been asked to dance a time or two! Me, at fifty-three years old, and I still get winks from the gentlemen every night.

It's no wonder I'm still here, I can't imagine another place I'd rather spend my working hours. Every day, I learn a bit more about life and, of course, death. But for most of these older folk, even death doesn't frighten them. The ones who know your love, Lord, are ready and even eager to be at the stepping-off place. May that I learn from them in this regard. In most every regard if the truth is told.

"Even to your old age, I shall be the same, and even to your graying years I shall bear you! I have done it, and I shall carry you; and I shall bear you, and I shall deliver you."
—ISAIAH 46:4

Dear Lord, I want to offer you my heart's gratitude for allowing me the privilege of ministering to these dear ones. I have learned so very much about life from each of them. Even when they are hurting and alone, the smallest of courtesies seems to arouse their spirit. Most often, I am amazed at how resilient these folks are. Almost every one has seen the death of a loved one, has had financial setbacks, illnesses that struck hard, and disappointments that took over. Still, they rally and tell me to look on the bright side. Perhaps it is the way that seasoned souls have of resigning themselves to expect both the good and the bad throughout life that impresses me. They are not pessimists, rather, they have learned that the rain falls on everyone. They've learned to rise above their circumstances. How I admire this courage. How I hunger for their wisdom and outlook. They are indeed courageous in my eyes.

Lord, I want to meet their needs effectively. I desire to come to these dear people with a loving heart each and every day. Give me your insight and your sensitivity so that I might understand how to best serve each individual I encounter. And, Lord, please make these meetings heavenly ones. Surely, there are a few who try my patience, but these are the exception. I've learned that as I give with a generous spirit, I am blessed all the more. With ears and eyes open, instruct my heart so that I am a living extension of your gracious care for these men and women who've endured so very much. Give me the words to lift up their spirits and help set their gaze once again upon your face. Lord, I thank you for this opportunity to glimpse beyond the earthly realms through the eyes of the more mature. Their unfaltering example gives me strength beyond telling. They are so often the mirrors of your unfailing love, and they have blessed me. Amen.

Treasures are everywhere. It's all in the knowing how and where to look.
—ANNETTE SMITH IN *Homemade Humble Pie*

48

Clean Hands

umping the waste into the bathroom toilet, Connie wrinkled her nose. Ugh, she involuntarily shuddered. Flushing the contents away, Connie's next task was to clean out the bedpan thoroughly. Then she had to give a sponge bath and put some more healing ointment on Mrs. Frayer's bedsores. Which reminded Connie to stop on the way home at the health food store and inquire about a better lotion that might speed up the healing process for her patient. Well, not really her "patient," but that's the way Connie felt about each man and woman who lived on Hall B, Connie's domain from 7:00 A.M. until 3:00 P.M. every weekday. Connie didn't have her R.N. certificate or a B.A. in nursing. But what Connie lacked in diplomas she more than made up for in heart. And Connie often thought, well, I do just about everything the day nurses do anyway.

By definition in the trade, Connie was a nurse's aide. But with the shortage of good help, caring help, Connie was sometimes expected to pitch in and assist with more than her share of the duties. But Connie didn't mind. She frequently told her friends that she felt called to this line of work. She didn't always like the unpleasantness that came part and parcel with caring for the human body. Still, Connie was devoted to her adopted grandmas and grandpas. She made special treats for those whose dietary restrictions allowed. Connie would take note of birthdays, anniversaries, even deaths and make sure she sent a card or took a few moments to converse and offer some comfort. It was no shock that Connie was one of the favorite employees around the home. But Connie never looked for recognition. She found her solace in quietly, gently, caring for those under her charge.

Make it your ambition to lead a quiet life and attend to your own business and work with your hands.
—1 Thessalonians 4:11

Dear Lord, today is a beautiful day. I welcome your presence into my heart even now. Lord, lift me up and place me on solid footing. Give me the good words I require to minister to those who are low and sick and without the comfort you so graciously supply. I ask that you provide me with the strength to serve. These, your eldest children, have come to a place in life where they depend upon others for their most basic needs. Let me attend to them with gentleness and care. Help me offer them the dignity and respect every person longs for. As I care for their needs, I pray that they see your unending love for them shine through. Indeed, I want to love these men and women with the caliber of your sacrificial love. You have set a standard for me. Please, enable me to give with the same lavishness that you demonstrated on a daily basis here on earth. No task is too humble for me to undertake, just as it was with Jesus. As my Lord, you have led the way to true servanthood. You held nothing back from those in need. Let my life be poured out in the same manner.

I welcome you into my world this day. Bring joy where there is no hope. Bring solace where there is no comfort. Bring peace where only fear resides. Lord, I ask that you fill me with your Holy Spirit and make me sensitive to your leading. Instruct me as I speak words of love to your people. Let your healing balm flow through me and nestle in the hearts of those I care for. I pray that today, no one will deny the grace, the eternal life you offer. Again, I ask that you supply me with your strength and give me what I need to make a difference today. In your name and for your sake, let me love these dear ones today. Amen.

Servants work for low pay, long hours, and no applause, "wasting" their talents and skills among the poor and uneducated. Somehow, though, in the process of losing their lives they find them.
—PHILIP YANCEY IN *The Jesus I Never Knew*

49

Confidential Concerns

*E*ileen and her husband, Joe, spent every Thursday evening and Saturday morning at the prison near their home. Before he retired, Joe had pastored a local church for over thirty years. Still eager to lend a helping hand in the community, Eileen and Joe jumped at the opportunity to lighten the current prison chaplain's heavy load. After a lengthy planning meeting and much prayer, they received permission to bring in a small group of their former parishioners and hold a "church" service of sorts for the men and women imprisoned here. Following some singing, Joe would teach a short Bible lesson, then the men would gather in a separate room with Joe and some other male volunteers. Eileen would spend the next hour with the female inmates.

It was during one of these meetings that Eileen discovered just how many regrets her new found friends were holding onto. Somehow—and it was amazing to Eileen, who never turned a hair after listening to the dreadful stories of abuse, rape, drug and alcohol addictions, and the like—these women just couldn't grasp how far God's love for each of them reached. Time and again, Eileen would open her Bible and share the tremendous hope that the gospel of Christ brings to every person who hears and believes. Still, these women were so hurt, so damaged, that they didn't believe it. "No one could love me after what I've done," said one woman after another. Eileen begged to differ. "I know what you've done, and I love you," she assured every woman present. It took months before the walls of distrust started to crumble. In Eileen's mind, it was worth every tear she privately shed for these ladies, every cookie she baked, every card she sent, every birthday she remembered, every small token of affection she extended. Eileen had it right: these women had to see and experience the genuineness of Eileen's love before they would entrust themselves to the love of an unseen savior.

Let the word of Christ richly dwell within you, with all wisdom teaching and admonishing one another with psalms and hymns and spiritual songs, singing with thankfulness in your hearts to God. And whatever you do in word or deed, do all in the name of the Lord Jesus, giving thanks through Him to God the Father.

—COLOSSIANS 3:16–17

Dear Lord, how can I thank you enough for extending our ministry into our later years? It is such a blessing to have the grand opportunities to share your unquenchable love with these dear, needy souls. I cannot express how honored I am to have this precious time with these special ones. I can see the possibilities. I know that you alone have given me the vision to see past their pain. You can heal their hearts. You, and only you, can heal their souls for eternity. Lord, this moment,

I ask you to begin a mighty work within their hearts. Slash through their resistance, open the way for your light to shine within them. Lord, give them that first sweet taste that forgiveness offers. Then let them drink from your well fully. As I share my heart, instruct me in the ways I can best communicate your love to them. Give me creative ideas to bring love to them in practical terms. Lord, I give you thanks for the great deeds you have already accomplished. I commit these hurting ones to your care and keeping. I ask that you, in your mercy, reach down and lift each one up to your bosom. Let not one reject eternal heaven because of the hell they've lived here on earth. Break through their barriers and give them new reason to live, new reason to rejoice. Amen.

> *The sick and the maimed are for us not hot spots of contamination but potential reservoirs of God's mercy. We are called upon to extend that mercy, to be conveyers of grace, not avoiders of contagion. Like Jesus, we can help make the "unclean" clean.*
> —PHILIP YANCEY IN *What's So Amazing About Grace?*

50
Right Aide

*F*our years earlier, Anna had taken over the management of her father's drugstore in their rural town. This was before all the large chains became the rage throughout the country. Anna understood the particular vision her father had for his store. Since her elementary school days, walking home included a quick side trip to Dad's store so he could hear an update of her escapades. These daily visits deepened an already close bond between father and daughter. Anna and her father had a relationship characterized by mutual respect, similar interests, and a sincere love for people. Anna's father was often seen dashing through their back door minutes before dinner was on the table because he had been assisting some elderly customer to her car, had helped change a flat tire for another patron, or an acquaintance of a friend simply needed some advice. All around town, Anna's father was widely regarded as the man to see if someone had a problem.

After Anna's dad died, no one in town was surprised to see Anna taking her father's place at the drugstore. Anna, now married with two children of her own, appeared to be picking up right where her father had left off. Her own two kids would scamper into the store on their way home from school. They would give her a quick update, ask for a sweet treat, and dash out again. At 5:00 P.M. sharp, Anna left the store each day in the capable hands of longtime employees. It never occurred to Anna to not continue sharing her dad's heritage of compassion and first-rate service to their community. She'd had too good an instructor and coach all those years. Anna saw it as a privilege to give.

On her way home each evening, Anna, just like her father, rehashed the day and made mental notes of any special needs she'd become aware of. She would make certain to follow up on the especially frail customers and send one of her trademark get-well flower bouquets with a card signed by the drugstore staff. Anna, having watched her dad, had learned well the fine art of serving the community.

Just as the son of Man did not come to be served, but to serve, and to give His life a ransom for many.
—MATTHEW 20:28

Dear Lord, I thank you for giving me such a family. It grieves me when I hear of how others mistreat or neglect their loved ones. I cannot fathom such behavior. This is the greatest blessing of all. For I learned to trust you through my dear one's example. He led me to a faith in you. His tender concern revealed your heart for your children.

I pray that you will give me the strength to continue giving to my community in the same way my loved one has done. Extend to me your compassion, your patience, and your mercy as I try to follow in these admirable footsteps. I was always taught to look beyond the outside of a person. My family showed me how to look within their hearts. Over the years, I've learned how to see past a person's brusque or rude demeanor. With prayer, you've given me a heart to give generously to even the most disagreeable. I thank you for passing along this vision to me that you bestowed upon my dear one. I want to pass this same burden of care onto my own children as they grow. Please Lord, as it was with my family, let unconditional love be the rule rather than the exception. Amen.

Christians must be willing to listen as much as they speak if they ever hope to be heard and taken seriously. Listening communicates more respect than speaking (a very hard task when you think you possess the truth). Listening suggests we may actually have something to learn.
—RICH NATHAN IN *Who Is My Enemy?*

51

Another Cup of Kindness, Please

*T*aking care not to chip the fine bone china inherited from her great aunt, Natalie cautiously removed the eight place settings from her china cabinet. It wasn't often that Natalie ventured to use these treasured dishes. But today was special. After weeks of planning, this afternoon at 2:00 P.M., seven of Natalie's neighbors would be joining her for tea. Normally a devout coffee drinker, Natalie had done some reading and learned how to properly prepare a nice sampling of teas for her guests. She'd also spent days planning the theme, the decorations, and the delicate tidbits of food she'd be serving. Natalie felt exhausted and excited all at once. A part of her was nervous, another part anticipated this long-awaited afternoon. It was no small matter to invite so many diverse personalities under one roof.

As she arranged the finger sandwiches on her serving platter, Natalie thought about why she was going to all this trouble. The idea of hosting an elegant tea party for women she hardly knew started after a short chat in the middle of the road. An acquaintance from the neighborhood was diagnosed with breast cancer, another woman was intent on divorcing her spouse, and still another had recently lost her mother in a car accident. On and on it went. Natalie had compassion for each of these ladies who suffered great loss. She felt compelled to try and ease the burdens they were carrying. Perhaps a quiet afternoon of pampering would lift their spirits. Natalie continued to attend to the details and looked at her watch again. Only twenty more minutes before they arrive. Now for the last preparation—prayer.

But thanks be to God, who always leads us in His triumph in Christ, and manifests through us the sweet aroma of the knowledge of Him in every place. For we are a fragrance of Christ to God among those who are being saved and among those who are perishing.

—2 CORINTHIANS 2:14–15

Dear Lord, I ask that you bless us with your presence. My prayer is that your exquisite love will permeate this place. I ask that you minister to our hearts. These special ones have all faced life's most difficult challenges and continue to fight. They are presently up against a host of problems and remain stalwart in their resistance against despair and depression. Please minister to each one according to her greatest need. I would ask that you touch the innermost soul and give every woman a new reason to rejoice. Let hope and joy dominate this day. Lord, you alone are able to renew the heart. Will you be my guest this day? I would have you at the place of highest honor at the head of my table. I invite you to share in our discussion and take part in our communion with one another. Let your goodness be evident to all. Allow me the privilege of serving these ladies in a manner worthy of you. Instruct my heart to encourage each one in just the right way. Give me the loving words that lift their hearts. And let each lady leave with a better knowledge of your great love for her personally. When this day is done, stay with my friends. Provide all that they need to conquer the obstacles in their lives and make them into strong women of faith who overcome. Somehow, Lord, break through any hearts that are full of complacency or despair. Open the hearts that are closed and let your embrace overpower any resistance to your love. Reckon with each of us today accordingly. Allow your Holy Spirit to do his grand work in his grand style. Let us bow before your throne in contriteness and humility as we recognize all your marvelous works accomplished on our behalf. Amen.

> *Our lives are sacred journeys along rocky paths, and sometimes we travel with stones in our shoes.*
> —WENDY MURRAY ZOBA IN *Sacred Journeys*

A Vow of Faith

*M*aureen sat alone in her dining room. Eyes closed, hands at her side, Maureen was laboring in prayer for the fifteen or so married women who came to her home every Tuesday evening to study the biblical foundations for transforming marriages. Nothing delighted Maureen more than to share the hope of God's constancy and care to women who felt their marriages were crumbling. Many of the ladies who entered Maureen's home were bereft of joy, no longer believing their futures held anything to look forward to. Some felt trapped in loveless relationships. Others were at an impasse with their respective spouses over hot-topic subjects. A few were simply bored. In her many years of serving as the leader and guide through these marriage studies, Maureen had seen it all. What used to stump Maureen, no longer did. Maureen had learned to unpack people's problems and break them into more manageable pieces. She taught women how to use the principles found in scripture to begin mending the rifts in their relationships.

What was so unique about Maureen was that she was not married. At one time, Maureen had taken a marriage vow. But after ten years of married life, her spouse decided that he wanted to be free of the restraints and responsibilities.

It was at that low point in Maureen's life that she began her own spiritual journey in search of healing and answers. Slowly, Maureen discovered biblical alternatives and remedies for women in troubled marriages. What Maureen learned and embraced has been the catalyst of powerful remedy for countless other hurting women. And Maureen wasn't one to give up or give in. Despite the obstacles in her friends' paths, Maureen would pray them through. She would gladly become the intercessor whom God continues to use. It was her greatest joy and privilege to take part in God's good work of transforming broken lives into strong, vibrant, and victorious showcases of his strength.

⌘

Give her the product of her hands,
And let her works praise her in the gates.
—PROVERBS 31:31

Dear Lord, I feel so very grateful for the solid foundation of hope and help that I can offer to my friends today. You know my history, my pain. And yet you've chosen to use me to offer help and hope to other hurting women. How novel and yet so like you, Lord! After these many years, I am astounded to find that I can continue to find new truths each and every day as I search the principles found in your word. There is nothing more I desire than to bring your good word to those who have been weakened by poor choices and downtrodden by the cares of the world. You alone know how greatly I suffered. During that time of pain and bereavement I thought I would never recover. Yet you were by my side, strengthening me, healing me, preparing me for this present task. Today, I am so honored to be able to share your good word of hope with these friends of mine. I am so fully confident of your healing power that I can speak with boldness about what you have accomplished in my own life.

Enable me now to speak with wisdom and to address specific problems with lasting solutions. Show me the path that brings glory and honor to the institution of marriage, Lord. Give us all the strength to do what pleases you rather than give in to retribution even when that retribution is well deserved. As we learn to trust in your ways, give us your strength and grace to make decisions that demonstrate our faith that you will continually provide. Open our eyes and let us see the good we can accomplish by looking to you as our comforter and guide. Grant us a resilient faith and open our tender hearts to receive the healing you so long to bestow on us. Amen.

Heavenly-mindedness is sanity. It is the best regimen for keeping our hearts whole, our minds clear. It allows us to enjoy earth's pleasures without debauchery. It allows us to endure life's agonies without despair.
—MARK BUCHANAN IN *Things Unseen*

Sources

Part One: Limited Resources

1 H. Jackson Brown Jr. and Rosemary C. Brown, *Life's Little Instructions from the Bible* (Nashville, Tenn.: Rutledge Hill Press, 2000), p. 130.

2 Joni Eareckson Tada with Steven Estes, *Christianity: A Follower's Guide* (Nashville, Tenn.: Broadman & Holman, 2001), p. 152.

3 Bruce Wilkinson, *Secrets of the Vine* (Sisters, Ore.: Multnomah, 2001), p. 18.

4 Philip Yancey, *The Jesus I Never Knew* (Grand Rapids, Mich.: Zondervan, 1995), p. 78.

5 Liz Curtis Higgs, *Bad Girls of the Bible* (Colorado Springs, Colo.: WaterBrook Press, 1999), p. 124.

6 Sheila Walsh, *Living Fearlessly* (Grand Rapids, Mich.: Zondervan, 2001), p. 26.

7 Carla Barnhill, *How to Parent Your Teen Without Losing Your Mind* (Nashville, Tenn.: Broadman & Holman, 2002), p. xv.

8 Anne Graham Lotz, *Just Give Me Jesus* (Nashville, Tenn.: Word, 2000), p. 43.

9 John Trent, *Be There!* (Colorado Springs, Colo.: WaterBrook Press, 2000), p. 48.

Part Two: Multitasking

10 Karen Scalf Linamen, *Sometimes I Wake Up Grumpy . . . and Sometimes I Let Him Sleep* (Grand Rapids, Mich.: Revell, 2001), p. 152.

11 Brian Schrauger, *Walking Taylor Home* (Nashville, Tenn.: W Publishing Group, 2001), p. 30.

12 James Emery White, *Life-Defining Moments* (Colorado Springs, Colo.: WaterBrook Press, 2001), p. 113.

13 Dave Burchett, *When Bad Christians Happen to Good People* (Colorado Springs, Colo.: WaterBrook Press, 2001), p. 20.

14 Susan Wilkinson, *Getting Past Your Past* (Sisters, Ore.: Multnomah, 2000), pp. 75–76.

15 Cynthia Spell Humbert, *Deceived by Shame* (Colorado Springs, Colo.: NavPress, 2001), p. 174.

16 Anne Graham Lotz, *Just Give Me Jesus* (Nashville, Tenn.: Word, 2000), p. 144.

17 A. W. Tozer, *Gems from Tozer* (Harrisburg, Pa.: Christian Publications, 1979), p. 71.

18 David Hazard, *Reducing Stress* (Eugene, Ore.: Harvest House, 2002), p. 55.

Part Three: Overcoming Obstacles and Discouragement

19 Bruce Nygren, *Touching the Shadows* (Nashville, Tenn.: Nelson, 2000), p. 144.

20 Fawn Parish, *It's All About You, Jesus* (Nashville, Tenn.: Nelson, 2001), p. x.

21 Bill Bright and Ted Dekker, *Blessed Child* (Nashville, Tenn.: W Publishing Group, 2001), p. 349.

22 Charles R. Swindoll, *Stress Fractures* (Sisters, Ore.: Multnomah, 1990), p. 244.

23 Charles Stanley, *How to Handle Adversity* (Nashville, Tenn.: Nelson, 1989), p. 138.

24 Philip Yancey, *What's So Amazing About Grace?* (Grand Rapids, Mich.: Zondervan, 1997), p. 273.

25 Joe White and Jim Weidmann (eds.), *Parents' Guide to the Spiritual Mentoring of Teens* (Carol Stream, Ill.: Tyndale House, 2001), p. 85.

26 Patricia S. Klein, *Worship Without Words* (Brewster, Mass.: Paraclete Press, 2000), p. xiii.

27 Stormie Omartian, *Lord, I Want to Be Whole* (Nashville, Tenn.: Nelson, 2000), p. 124.

28 Sharon Marshall with Jeff Johnson, *Take My Hand* (Grand Rapids, Mich.: Zondervan, 2001), p. 39.

29 Grace Ketterman and David Hazard, *When You Can't Say "I Forgive You"* (Colorado Springs, Colo.: NavPress, 2000), p. 110.

30 Janet Holm McHenry, *PrayerWalk* (Colorado Springs, Colo.: WaterBrook Press, 2001), p. 96.

31 Larry Crabb, *The Pressure's Off* (Colorado Springs, Colo.: WaterBrook Press, 2002), p. 75.

Part Four: Facing Fears

32 Larry Crabb, *Secrets of a Faith Well Lived* (West Monroe, La.: Howard, 2001), p. 98.

33 Charles Stanley, *A Gift of Love* (Nashville, Tenn.: Nelson, 2001), p. 41.

34 Max Lucado, *Traveling Light* (Nashville, Tenn.: Word, 2001), p. 164.

35 Joe White and Jim Weidmann (eds.), *Parents' Guide to the Spiritual Mentoring of Teens* (Carol Stream, Ill.: Tyndale House, 2001), p. 38.

36 Jerry White, *Making Peace with Reality* (Colorado Springs, Colo.: NavPress, 2002), p. 191.

37 Barbara Johnson, *God's Most Precious Jewels Are Crystallized Tears* (Nashville, Tenn.: Word, 2001), p. 56.

38 Jeannie St. John Taylor, *How to Be a Praying Mom* (Peabody, Mass.: Hendrickson, 2001), p. 31.

39 Calvin Miller, *Jesus Loves Me* (New York: Warner Books, 2002), p. 77.

40 Jean Lush with Pam Vredevelt, *Women and Stress* (Grand Rapids, Mich.: Revell, 1992), p. 263.

41 David Hansen, *Long Wandering Prayer* (Downers Grove, Ill.: InterVarsity Press, 2001), p. 100.

Part Five: Discovering Joy and Satisfaction

42 Donna VanLiere, *The Christmas Shoes* (New York: St. Martin's Press, 2001), p. 115.

43 Cynthia Heald, *In the Secret Place of the Most High* (Nashville, Tenn.: Nelson, 2001), pp. vii–viii.

44 Sheila Walsh, *A Love So Big* (Colorado Springs, Colo.: WaterBrook Press, 2002), p. 52.

45 Donald. S. Whitney, *Ten Questions to Diagnose Your Spiritual Health* (Colorado Springs, Colo.: NavPress, 2001), p. 90.

46 Michael W. Smith, *I Will Be Your Friend* (Nashville, Tenn.: Nelson, 2001), p. 89.

47 Annette Smith, *Homemade Humble Pie* (Grand Rapids, Mich.: Revell, 2001), p. 161.

48 Philip Yancey, *The Jesus I Never Knew* (Grand Rapids, Mich.: Zondervan, 1995), p. 118.

49 Philip Yancey, *What's So Amazing About Grace?* (Grand Rapids, Mich.: Zondervan, 1997), p. 155.

50 Rich Nathan, *Who Is My Enemy?* (Grand Rapids, Mich.: Zondervan, 2002), p. 34.

51 Wendy Murray Zoba, *Sacred Journeys* (Carol Stream, Ill.: Tyndale House, 2002), p. 191.

52 Mark Buchanan, *Things Unseen* (Sisters, Ore.: Multnomah, 2002), p. 18.

The Author

*M*ichele Howe lives in LaSalle, Michigan, with her husband and four children, where she has been homeschooling for twelve years. She is a book reviewer for *Publishers Weekly, CBA Marketplace,* and *CCM Magazine.* Michele has published over seven hundred articles and reviews and is the author of several books, including *Going It Alone: Meeting the Challenges of Being a Single Mom* and *Pilgrim Prayers for Single Mothers*

Prayers for Homeschool Moms

Michele Howe

$12.95 Hardcover

ISBN: 0-7879-6557-X

"Michele Howe presents realistic struggles and scenarios home educators can relate to all too well, then takes them by the hand and leads them to the ideal response: intimate dialogue with Jesus. Prepare to be challenged, convicted, comforted, even contemplative, as you pray the prayers of a homeschool mom."

> —**Ann Kroeker**, author of *The Contemplative Mom: Restoring Rich Relationship with God in the Midst of Motherhood*

"Amazingly, Howe addresses every single issue that confronts homeschooling mothers today: each apprehension and thrill, each struggle and triumph. There is a prayer for all of us in this book."

> —**Kristyn Komarnicki**, editor, *PRISM Magazine* and homeschooling mother of three boys

"Michele Howe has not left one stone unturned in this vast compilation of life stories and prayers from moms in the homeschooling community. In *Prayers for Homeschool Moms,* Mrs. Howe guides us from the surface tensions of our lives into the inner sanctum of prayer and hope, reminding us that we are never alone."

> —**Susan Card**, author of *The Homeschool Journey*

This wonderful gift book provides emotional support for those who are balancing the multiple pressures of being a good mom, a good teacher, and a good wife, all from the heart of one seasoned homeschool mom to another. For the mom who is often so overwhelmed by her circumstances that she can't think straight, this book provides welcomed relief, inspiration, and hope through its "teaching" stories—stories that show the inspiring successes of other homeschoolers.

Michele Howe is a book reviewer for *Publishers Weekly, CBA Marketplace,* and *CCM Magazine.* Michele has published over 700 articles and reviews and is the author of several books including *Prayers to Nourish a Woman's Heart* and *Prayers of Comfort and Strength.* She lives with her husband and children near Grand Rapids, Michigan. [Price subject to change]